Happy 40th Birthday,

To my Dear friend

May you have a great year,

Happiness thru out your life. You

are a very special friend to have

Many Happy Birthday's
to come !!

Love ya,

Bonnie

SIMPLE PATH

to relaxation

SIMPLE PATH

to relaxation

Anthea Courtenay

MQP

First published by MQ Publications Limited
12 The Ivories, 6–8 Northampton Street
London N1 2HY

Senior Editor **Roz Hopkins**
Editor **Jenni Davies**
Designer **Justina Leitão**
Picture Researcher **Suzie Green**

ISBN: 1-84072-306-8

Printed in China

Contents

INTRODUCTION

why relax?

> *"… still the Queen kept crying 'Faster, faster!'*
> *but Alice felt she could not go faster, though she had*
> *no breath left to say so. …*
> *'Now, here, you see, it takes all the running you can*
> *do to keep in the same place.'"*

Lewis Carroll, *Through the Looking-Glass*

It is hardly news that modern society is suffering increasingly from tension and stress. Life around us seems to be speeding up, and adults, trying to keep pace, are becoming more and more prone to stress-related illnesses. Children, too, are feeling stressed; in one recent study more than a quarter of a group of British children aged seven and upward said they felt stressed all the time.

The natural reaction is often to drive oneself harder to keep up. But trying too hard for too long has its costs, to our health, to our relationships, and to our sense of self.

Many people are striving for a more natural approach to life—organic foods and natural medicines, for example, are growing in popularity. What tends to be forgotten, though, is that relaxation is also a necessary part of our daily life cycle, just as eating is. All living things go through cycles of activity followed by rest and recuperation; only humans try to carry on with insufficient rest.

Incorporating relaxation into the daily rhythm of life can only improve our physical health, mental efficiency, and emotional well-being. This book looks at some methods of relaxing not only your body, but also your attitudes.

What stops you relaxing?

One reason many people find it hard to relax is that they put up mental barriers to the very idea. Do any of the following statements ring a bell with you?

❀ If I stop to relax, I'll never get everything done.

❀ My parents were always busy and brought me up to use every minute of the day.

❀ Doing nothing is a waste of time.

❀ I don't really know what it feels like to be relaxed.

❀ I have a busy job/home life—taking time to relax is self-indulgent!

❀ If I become a relaxed person I'll be less efficient/hard-nosed at work.

❀ I'm afraid of letting go.

Objections like these may be part of your conditioned beliefs, and it's a good idea to stand back and take a look at them. Are they based on reality? As you will see from the ideas and facts put forward in this book, and from some of the personal stories quoted, they certainly don't have to be. In fact, it's when we are over-stressed that we function less efficiently, make careless mistakes, and snap at our nearest and dearest.

Properly practiced and incorporated into your lifestyle, relaxation—besides being an extremely pleasant way to spend some of your time—will add to your efficiency and clarity of mind. Far from "doing nothing," it is a way of putting your body and mind into a state in which you can live more effectively and happily. Nor is there anything selfish about this: looking after yourself ultimately means that you have more of yourself to give to others.

case study wanting it all—and getting it

Anita was a young, highly talented, and successful violinist, happily married with a caring husband who supported her career, which included teaching the violin as well as playing with an orchestra at concerts around the world. She was a compulsive over-achiever, however, living her life at frenetic top speed.

A few years ago Anita desperately wanted to have a child, while still continuing her career; instead, she suffered the disappointment of three early miscarriages.

A friend, a fellow musician, was able to see Anita more clearly than she could see herself; he recognized that her efforts to give of her best as musician, teacher, and potential mother were making her very tense. He suggested that she visit Beth, a relaxation therapist whose work he had experienced himself. Anita decided she had nothing to lose, and made an appointment to see Beth. After talking with Anita and discussing at length her lifestyle and attitudes, Beth showed her how to enter into a relaxed state, and Anita found herself able to acknowledge for the first time the extreme state of tension she had been living in.

During the course of therapy that followed their first meeting, Beth showed Anita a number of ways of relaxing the body and mind. She recorded three tapes for Anita to take away and work with in her own time—one on simple body relaxation, one on meditation, and one on breathing. Anita's perfectionist approach to life paid off here: with the help of the tapes she practiced her relaxation techniques regularly and diligently.

It worked. Within the year Anita was pregnant again, and this time she had a beautiful baby. She now has three happy, healthy children—and is still both playing and teaching the violin. Interestingly, her students and colleagues quite soon noticed that her teaching style began to change: she gave more time to listening to her students individually and encouraging them as they progressed, rather than simply pouncing on their mistakes and demanding immediate perfection! Her students, not surprisingly, said they much preferred her new way of being with them, and Anita was rewarded by seeing their positive response.

What is interesting about this story is that as a result of taking relaxation seriously, Anita did not stop achieving—in fact she achieved very much more, but in a different way. She was still working and teaching as before, and she had her longed-for family, but she was now free of the self-imposed stress she had been suffering from for so long. The change in her approach to teaching came about not as a conscious decision, but as a natural result of the changes that had taken place within her own being.

Beth, Anita's therapist, explains that "the repeated practice of relaxation eventually permanently changes the nervous system's responses to stress. This is not to say that you never experience stress—just that the nervous system doesn't jump to attention quite so quickly. But you don't lose your ability to evaluate situations—in fact you usually increase it."

This is echoed by both men and women in high-powered jobs, who have found that incorporating relaxation into their lives has made them more effective, not less, while creative people feel more in touch with their creativity.

How relaxation works

Most people are familiar with the term "fight or flight," which describes the body's immediate physiological response to a stressful situation. In an extreme case the heart begins to race, the palms grow sweaty, the stomach churns uncontrollably, and you may find yourself trembling, or perhaps even feeling faint. This is because stress acts on one branch of the sympathetic nervous system to produce hormones in the body, particularly adrenaline and non-adrenaline, which are automatically released to prepare you to deal with the situation— either to fight whatever you are up against, or to flee from it. In prehistoric times, faced with a bear or an antagonistic tribe, this response was totally appropriate, and the adrenaline served a positive purpose in gearing up the body to take action.

These days, most of us cannot respond in either of these natural ways: however stressed we may be in our offices, in bus lines, by our managers, colleagues, children, or partners, we are nevertheless unable to fight or flee. Though the modern phenomenon of "road rage" and other rages implies that some people actually do become stressed enough to abandon their social conditioning, most people somehow manage to suppress their instinctive reactions even in an extremely stressful situation.

In fact, Vera Diamond, a teacher of Autogenic Relaxation (see page 145) points out that people don't always realize that there is a third strand to this mechanism, "It's fight, flight, or freeze!" A lot of people get paralyzed—you are frozen and you can't cope, and can't get it together. That's the same syndrome. It's not as obvious, it's more subtle—but it's devastating."

To strive for a completely stress-free existence is unrealistic, and in fact a little stress is necessary to life, keeping us alert and motivated as we go about our daily tasks. However, prolonged, unresolved stress creates a build-up of stress hormones, which can lead to ill-health and to even more anxiety. Among its effects are a lowered immune system, which in turn leads to a greater susceptibility to infectious or genetic diseases; high blood pressure, which can lead to cardiac arrests and strokes; migraine, indigestion, insomnia, irritability, anger, and depression. Allergic responses such as eczema and asthma are exacerbated. At the same time, muscles constantly held tight in tension can lead to aching shoulders, neck and back, headaches, poor posture, arthritis, and fatigue.

Relaxation not only stops this process, but actually reverses it. Letting go, mentally and physically, brings into play another branch of the sympathetic nervous system, called the parasympathetic. This releases some of the more kindly hormones into the bloodstream, counteracting the effects of stress and strengthening the immune system. When the body is in a deep state of relaxation, neurotransmitters in the brain, called endorphins, are produced, creating a much more pleasant sensation in both body and mind, and helping to relieve pain. In addition, relaxed muscles benefit from the improved bloodflow, which is hindered by tension, and the rested body has more energy to renew its tasks.

There are, obviously, numerous health benefits to this, as the physiological effects of stress are reversed—and some of them are less obvious. Anita is not the only person whose fertility problems have been solved following a course of relaxation. And there can be powerful effects on the mind, and on one's outlook on life.

What happens in the brain

When the body enters a relaxed state, two important things happen in the brain. Firstly, the brainwaves slow down from the beta rhythm, which governs our normal everyday functioning, to slower rhythms known as alpha and theta waves; these brainwaves are those associated with creative activity and with the calm, peaceful states experienced in meditation.

At the same time, the two halves of the brain begin to function more harmoniously. Our brains are divided in two, with a connection down the middle—rather like a walnut. The left side deals primarily with speech and logical, practical thinking, and in many people it tends to be overused at the expense of the right side, which deals with imagery, dreams, creativity, and feelings. Deep relaxation synchronizes the two halves, giving the right side a chance to come into play, creating a better emotional balance. This is one reason why letting go of our anxieties, even if only for a short while, can help with any issues that are causing us concern—as soon as we stop hanging on to the problem, the best and often the most obvious solution often bubbles up of its own accord.

The emotions

Learning to experience inner peace, and gaining the ability to enter that state when you want to, actually gives you more control over your emotional responses when you return to the fray. Over time, as we saw in Anita's case, people often become more tolerant and laid back, without losing their effectiveness, and are generally happier all round. As well as possibly living longer, you become a nicer person for others to live with!

One fear people have about relaxing is that, if they let go of their mental control, emotional traumas or bad memories may surface. This is very unlikely to happen if you are practicing a fairly light method of relaxation on your own. To reach the very deep state in which unconscious memories are accessed, you need to work with a therapist. In fact, deep relaxation can help to access such memories without necessarily experiencing the original anguish, and can help you to look at them and heal them, particularly with the help of a good therapist. This is the state that hypnotherapists use, not only to access memories, but to help the client to use visualization to improve his or her health. For this self-healing process to work, the brain and body have to be in a simultaneously receptive state, as do the brain and the autonomic nervous system—the part of our nervous system that is usually beyond conscious control.

A skill to be learned

Relaxation is, unfortunately, a skill that many people have to learn, or relearn. Once you start experiencing its benefits, you can choose how far you want to take it. You can safely practice the exercises in the early part of the book on your own. But if you have problems reaching a relaxed state you may need help, either from a hands-on therapist, or by joining a class or group. You may also need to take a serious look at your lifestyle; chapter five suggests some ways in which you can change your everyday behavior and attitudes.

We are all different, and some suggestions in this book may appeal more to some people than others. One of the benefits of practicing relaxation is that you develop more self-awareness, and may also increase your ability to discover and follow what is right for you.

Are you a
Type A
or a Type B?

In the 1970s two American cardiologists, M. Friedman and R. H. Roseman, discovered that a relationship existed between personality, stress, and heart disease. From their subsequent researches into the connection, Friedman and Roseman divided people into two categories. An extreme Type A is go-getting, ambitious, time-conscious, and achievement oriented—the archetypal busy executive. He or she is twice as likely to suffer from heart disease as an extreme Type B, who is far more placid, easy-going, unhurried, patient, and unruffled by disaster.

Most of us are somewhere between these extremes. But it seems likely that the reason for the increased number of cardiac arrests current among women is that in order to succeed in a male preserve, possibly running a home and family at the same time, a woman has to be, or learn to be, more Type A than a man.

Which category do you belong to?

If you are an extreme Type A you are unlikely to be reading this book, and if you are a complete Type B you simply won't feel the need to. Most people are a mixture of the two, and tend to adopt Type A behavior in a crisis.

Much Type A behavior has been learned, and can be modified—though an extreme Type A will need a strong motivation to change.

Most **Type A** people have at least six of the following traits:

❀ Excessive competitiveness—must win at everything.

❀ Aggressiveness.

❀ Impatience: has difficulty in listening, hates standing in line.

❀ Easily roused to anger.

❀ Easily irritated even over small matters.

❀ Constantly trying to meet self-imposed deadlines.

❀ Lives life at top speed; eats, speaks, and drives fast.

❀ Time urgency, driving themselves and others to achieve more and more.

❀ Insecurity, lacking self-esteem.

❀ Unrealistically high expectations of themselves.

❀ Difficulty in giving and receiving love.

❀ Fascination with numbers.

❀ Lacking in imagery, speech lacks metaphors and similes.

❀ Smoking.

❀ Frequent swearing.

❀ Desire to dominate situations.

❀ Frequent sighing.

❀ Inability to sit still and do nothing.

❀ Criticism of others, creating guilt and sense of failure if demands cannot be met.

Most **Type B** people have at least six of the following traits:

✿ No sense of time urgency.

✿ Ability to take the long view.

✿ Enjoyment of contemplation.

✿ Lacking in free-floating hostility.

✿ No wish to control others or situations.

✿ Knowing what to disregard.

✿ Ability to overlook other people's shortcomings.

✿ Ability to give and receive love.

✿ Good self-esteem.

✿ Unhurried in speech, movement, and eating.

✿ A humble outlook.

✿ Ability to listen, patience with others.

✿ Understanding and compassion.

CHAPTER ONE

getting started

> **66** *If a man insisted always on being serious,*
> *and never allowed himself*
> *a bit of fun and relaxation,*
> *he would go mad or become unstable*
> *without knowing it.* **99**
>
> Herodotus

Before you start learning to relax, you need to make a serious appointment with yourself—and with anyone you live with—and set aside a time when you won't be disturbed. If you know you are half-expecting a phone call, or someone in the family is going out and is likely to demand that you help find their favorite sweater, you simply will not be able to relax properly. Make this *your* time, and if possible keep to it regularly, so that everyone gets used to the idea and knows that there are times when you are not to be disturbed. If you have never consciously relaxed before, you will be embarking on a path that could change your health and your life for the better. Try to program into your week at least three sessions of 20–30 minutes. Since these will be enjoyable minutes, this should not cause you too much of an effort.

Read this next section right through before you start practicing. Dress comfortably in loose clothing, and gather together any "props" you might need, such as soothing music or candles. Then find yourself a space where you can both move and lie down—probably your bedroom—and close the door firmly on the outside world.

Exercise the body

Exercise is an excellent way of encouraging good breathing and generally putting you in a satisfying state of calm and well-being. It is also a great stress-reducer, helping to put to good use those "fight or flight" hormones—without having a confrontation with anyone!—so it is an ideal way to end a stressful day at work, for example.

If your focus is on relaxation, choose noncompetitive and enjoyable types of exercise like swimming, walking, and dancing (salsa is great for using the whole body and lifting the spirits), which will not only loosen up your body but encourage full, deep breathing. If you prefer a structured approach, try going to a class where you will be guided in a more formal type of exercise such as pilates, yoga, t'ai chi, or chi kung, described on pages 156-203.

Warming down exercises

If you are unused to spending time in total relaxation, you will probably find it difficult to let go all at once—very often your mind will be cluttered with distracting thoughts about something that's happened during the day, or an urgent task that needs to be dealt with, while your body is equally determined to hold on to tension from sitting for hours at your computer or driving in heavy peak-hour traffic. It's very helpful to begin any relaxation session with some physical movement that will release all the tensions, and slow down the body and mind.

On the following pages are some "warming down" exercises that will focus your attention on unwinding, so that you will be in the right frame of mind to get the most out of your relaxation session. Try them out to see which suits you best.

SWINGING

✿ Stand with your feet shoulder-width apart, and your toes facing forward.

✿ Keep your knees slightly bent rather than locked, and hold your arms loosely by your sides.

✿ Now swing from side to side, letting the movement come from the waist, slightly bending each knee in turn as your weight falls on it.

✿ Begin this swing fairly fast. You will find your arms swinging naturally from the shoulders and around your body, with your hands lightly slapping your sides and back.

✿ Now gradually slow down, so that your arms swing less widely, continuing to bend alternate knees as you turn. You will find this swing very soothing.

STRETCHING

✿ Stand with your feet shoulder-width apart.

✿ Stretch your arms upward and outward while you breathe in, increasing the stretch as much as you can.

✿ As you breathe out, let your arms flop and your shoulders drop.

NECK AND HEAD ROLLING

✿ Standing as before, let your head drop forward.

✿ Slowly turn it toward the left shoulder, so that the right side of your neck is stretched.

✿ Bring your head forward and round to the right, so that the left side of your neck is stretched.

✿ Repeat 4–5 times.

SHOULDER HUNCHING

✿ Most people carry a lot of tension in their shoulders. Ease this by bringing your shoulders as high as you can toward your ears, holding them there for a moment, and then letting them completely relax and drop.

✿ Repeat this about 5 times.

SHOULDER ROLLING AND HAND RELEASING

✿ Standing with your feet shoulder-width apart, and your arms hanging loose, rotate your shoulders backward 10 times, and then forward 10 times.

✿ Now, keeping your hands and wrists floppy, shake out your forearms. As you do this, imagine you are shaking from your fingers any unwanted stress from your day.

ROLLING ON THE FLOOR

❀ Put on a tape or CD of some relaxing music.

❀ Lie on the floor and start by curling up in a ball with your arms round your knees.

❀ Roll from side to side a few times, to give your spine a massage.

❀ Then, roll around more freely to the music, stretching your arms, legs, and spine.

❀ From here you can move directly into a lying-down relaxation, keeping the music going if it suits you.

IMPROVISING

❀ You may prefer to move and stretch in a less structured way, by putting on some music and letting your body move to it as it wants, getting ready to let go for the whole-body relaxation.

Relaxation
routines

Allow yourself at least 15 minutes to go through the routines described here and on pages 40-43: as you learn to relax, you may well find yourself wanting more. Either read through the instructions several times beforehand, or tape record them in advance, so that you don't have to disturb yourself by checking that you're "getting it right."

If you're worried about timing, keep a clock where you can see it, or tell yourself beforehand that you have 10, 15, or 20 minutes—trust your inner clock, and you should find yourself naturally ending your session at the time you have decided on.

Begin by lying down. Tempting though it may be to lie on your bed, it is best to use the floor, which will give your body better support. If you like, fold a blanket to lie on. Place a small cushion or thick book under your head. If you have a lower back problem, a pillow under your knees will help to prevent strain.

ROUTINE 1: TENSE AND RELAX

This routine helps you to recognize the difference between tense and relaxed muscles as you become familiar with the sensations of relaxing.

❀ Lie down on your back, with your arms an inch or two away from your sides and your palms turned upward. Your feet should be a few inches apart; let your feet and ankles fall naturally outward.

❀ Breathe slowly and deeply, without forcing your breath. As you breathe in, clench your hands as hard as you can, feeling the tension right up to your shoulders. As you breathe out, let them go.

❀ Breathe in and stretch your fingers as far and wide as you can. Breathe out and let them go.

❀ Breathe in and curl your toes as hard as you can, so that you feel the tension all the way up your legs. Breathe out and let them go.

✿ Breathe in and screw up all your face muscles as tightly as you can, frown, clench the jaw, tighten your neck muscles. Breathe out and let your facial muscles go, and allow your jaw to drop naturally.

✿ Breathe in and stiffen the whole body from head to toe. Breathe out, and let go completely.

✿ Continue to lie there. If you notice any particular areas of tension, repeat the process of tensing up and letting go. Then, for the next few minutes, allow yourself to enjoy lying there, completely at rest.

COMING OUT

✿ Slowly come back to the everyday world. Wriggle your fingers and toes, and stretch your arms and legs. Yawn if you feel like it. Roll on to your side, then on to your hands and knees, so that you return to standing from a kneeling position. Have another good stretch.

ROUTINE 2: **RELAXING THE WHOLE BODY**

You may find it helpful to prerecord this exercise on tape. You will be giving different parts of your body instructions to relax: don't make yourself relax, but allow your body to respond naturally to your mind.

Prepare yourself with some warming-down movements and lie on the floor as before, with your hands by your sides, palms upward. Close your eyes.

❀ Begin by being aware of your whole body lying on the floor. Be aware of the floor beneath you, supporting your back, supporting your whole body. Breathe and relax.

❀ Turn your attention to your head and scalp. Tell yourself, "I am relaxing, I am letting go." Breathe easily, deeply, and calmly.

❀ Let your attention go to your brow and your eyes, and think of releasing any tension there. "I am relaxing my forehead, I am relaxing my eyes." Breathe and relax.

✿ Let your awareness move to your face and jaw. "I am relaxing my face and jaw."

✿ Let your jaw drop a little, naturally, your tongue resting on the floor of your mouth. Breathe easily, calmly, and deeply.

✿ Take your attention to your neck, telling yourself, "My neck muscles are soft and loose." Breathe and relax.

✿ Move down to your shoulders, telling yourself, "My shoulders are letting go." Breathe easily and deeply.

✿ Be aware of the top of your chest, and imagine it expanding. "My chest is opening and expanding." Breathe and relax.

✿ Be aware of your upper back, and feel it expanding. "My upper back is expanding and relaxing." Breathe easily, deeply, and calmly.

❀ Be aware of your lower back, and let any tension in it loosen. "My lower back is relaxing and resting." Breathe and relax.

❀ Be aware of your thighs, front and back. "My thighs are relaxing and letting go of tension." Breathe easily, deeply, and calmly.

❀ Be aware of your knees, back and front. "My knees are relaxing and letting go." Breathe and relax.

❀ Be aware of your legs from your knees to your ankles. "My legs are relaxing and letting go." Breathe easily, deeply, and calmly.

❀ Be aware of your feet and ankles, and let go of any tension. "My ankles and feet are relaxing and resting." Breathe and relax.

❀ Notice how relaxed your whole body feels. Let any remaining tension go, breathing in and out with an awareness of the tension.

❀ Continue to tell yourself to breathe and relax. Tell yourself, "With each breath, I am becoming more deeply relaxed."

❀ Allow yourself to enjoy the sensation of being deeply relaxed. Your mind may feel dreamy, and your body may feel very heavy, or possibly light and "floaty." You may feel a warmth and tingling in your hands and feet. Take note of any sensations; you are training your body/mind to recognize what it feels like to be relaxed.

If you notice your stomach gurgling more than usual, it shows that the relaxation is reaching your digestive system and encouraging the process of peristalsis, by which food is pushed through the gut.

COMING OUT

Come out as described for Routine 1—wriggle your hands and toes, and get up slowly. Feel your feet fully on the ground, and make sure that you are totally alert before you start any other activities.

A word about breathing

Under stress most people tend to take short, shallow breaths—very often people hold their breath at anxious moments. Begin to notice whether you do this, and every time you catch yourself holding your breath, sigh out and let go.

We are not meant to breathe shallowly: watch a baby or an animal breathing, and you will see that the breath naturally moves the whole body—not only the ribs but the sides, the stomach, and even the back are in gentle motion. Yet by the time we are adults, most of us have acquired diminished breathing habits, usually breathing in the middle of the chest only.

Our lungs fill a surprisingly large area of the chest from close to our shoulders down to our diaphragm, and they are meant to be used. They have the important function of circulating oxygen through the bloodstream, to feed our muscles, organs, and brains. Breath is life, and in Eastern health systems it is associated with the intake not just of air, but of the life force—prana in Yoga and Indian medicine, chi in Chinese medicine and martial arts.

Deep, slow, calm breathing is an essential component of relaxation. Pay attention to your breathing rhythm and allow it to slow down and become deeper naturally. A relaxation expert comments: "Conscious breathing is beautifully calming and centering. But I don't teach techniques. Doing exercises can help if you need to learn to expand your lungs, but that's also imposing a pattern onto what is there.

"Depressed people actually tend to breathe out too much, so they're not oxygenating the brain, but most people focus on breathing in instead of breathing out. If you breathe out first, breathing in is like the rebound of a ball, and has a totally different dynamic. Many people hold their breath when they're anxious or in pain; breathing out can release both pain and tension. Holding your breath stems from fear; it's like preparing for something, and then not doing it."

Some relaxation teachers stress the importance of diaphragmatic breathing; others focus on abdominal breathing. The difference is probably more to do with where you focus your attention than with the actual movement of your breath. We cannot, of course, literally breathe through the abdomen, but allowing the diaphragm to be used more fully will also enable the abdomen to rise and fall. You may like to try both out, either lying down, or sitting comfortably in a chair. If sitting, have your back supported and your legs uncrossed, feet on the ground. You can practice these as calming techniques during the day.

Always breathe in through the nose. You can breathe out through nose or mouth; see which feels more comfortable to you. And follow your own natural breathing rhythm.

DIAPHRAGMATIC BREATHING

✿ Place your hands over your diaphragm so that the fingertips of each hand overlap.

✿ Place your attention on your lower ribs and allow the breath to expand them. Feel the ribs widening outward.

✿ As you breathe in, the overlapping fingertips will naturally draw away from each other, leaving a gap.

✿ Breathe like this for a minute or two, enjoying the sensation of expansion and contraction in your diaphragm and rib cage.

ABDOMINAL BREATHING

This is favored in Eastern methods of relaxation. "Unforced, comfortable abdominal breathing is the fastest way into relaxation," according to a relaxation therapist. "It is just the natural breath, which most people don't access."

❀ Place your hands over your lower abdomen.

❀ Allow each breath you take to become deeper and slower.

❀ As you breathe in, imagine that the breath is filling your lower belly. Don't force it, simply direct it with your thoughts.

❀ As you breathe out, let your abdomen relax (forget about having a flat stomach for the time being!)

Whichever method you favor, don't lose touch with the upper part of your chest and lungs; the whole torso should be engaged.

Exercise the mind

As you become used to the sensation of relaxing, there are ways in which you can deepen your relaxation experience. There are numerous tapes and CDs on the market by therapists and healers, which can be very helpful; it is often easier to let go to the sound of someone else's voice. The only drawback is that the speaker's rhythm and timing may not be the same as yours.

You can also create your own scenarios by adding imagery and sensation, using the whole-body relaxation as a basis. You may find it helpful to play some soothing music, or a New Age tape specially composed as a background to meditation and relaxation. When visualizing, don't worry if you don't have a very clear image, and don't strain for one. Simply enjoy the experience.

The sea

A visit to a deserted seashore very early in the morning, when the rising sun is just starting to cast a sparkle on the waves as they gently lap against the sand, is a totally relaxing experience. It is one that is easy to recall later, perhaps because the scene is so simple—a calm sea and the fresh, pale-blue sky stretching away until they meet on the horizon, a flat expanse of yellow sand washed clean by the water, perhaps the vague outline of a misty mountain as a backdrop, and nothing more. Sit on the sand and close your eyes, feeling the warmth of the sun—the sounds will be easy to recall, too, just the ebb and flow of the waves, coming and going slowly and rhythmically, like your breath. Even the harsh cry of a seagull is evocative.

Visit your favorite shore, or study a wonderful picture or photograph that appeals to you, and hold the image in your mind as the basis for your visualization.

Begin by lying down and letting the whole body relax.

❀ Imagine that you are standing on the shore by the sea. It is a beautiful day, comfortably hot, and the sun is catching the surface of the waves so that they sparkle in the light. As you stand there, watch the waves gently coming in and out in their eternal, natural motion. Listen to their soothing sound as they flow forward onto the beach and pull back. Feel the sand under your bare feet.

❀ Step into the water and feel it lapping round your feet, ankles, and legs. The water is warm and friendly. Walk further in, enjoying the sensation of the water round your feet, legs, and ankles, your thighs and your body, until the water is up to your shoulders.

❀ Now you can let go and allow the sea to support you. Let yourself float comfortably and safely, sensing the water holding you up. Above you the sky is a deep clear blue and there are small white clouds floating across it. You can see the beach and, beyond it, beautiful mountains, their snowy peaks lit by the sun.

❀ Know that you are quite safe, the sea is your friend and will hold you up. Feel your body gently and rhythmically rocked by the waves. As you float there, you are aware that you are becoming at one with the sea, at one with its rhythm and beauty. Relax and let yourself go; enjoy the sensation of being at one with the ocean.

❀ When you know it is time to return to the shore, imagine yourself turning over and swimming back with strong, powerful strokes. Your body feels light and energized. As you step out of the water, feel the sand again under your feet and toes. Take a last look at the ocean before opening your eyes and coming back to the room.

❀ Stretch, move your hands and feet, yawn if you feel like it, and get up slowly, making sure your feet are firmly planted on the ground.

Being an animal

Last summer, on a visit to a wildlife park, I watched a snowleopard lying full stretch on the branch of a tree: this was one of the most powerful images of relaxation I have ever seen. He was dozing, eyes tightly shut, uninhibited and totally oblivious to the activities of the rest of the world below him, with one paw, usually so full of strength and power, flopping limply over the side of the branch. You may have seen similar wild animals in a state of rest, or even your own cat or dog splayed out on the rug in a shaft of sunlight, in the complete ecstasy of letting go. The art of relaxation definitely comes more naturally to animals than it does to humans!

For this session, choose an image that is personal to you—you may have experienced a similar sight, or seen a photograph of an animal at rest and wished you could emulate its ability to let go—and fill in your own details.

✿ Begin your relaxation in the usual way for a few minutes. Then bring to your mind the image of the animal you have chosen. Visualize its surroundings—the trees, the grass, and the color of the sky, or a quiet room lit by the sun or by a log fire burning lazily in the hearth. Now visualize the surface the animal is lying on—a safe, sturdy branch, a soft rug, or a plump cushion in a basket. Appreciate the animal's beauty, its color, its sleek muscles, the sheen of its fur, its beautiful markings.

✿ When you have a clear picture in your mind, choose to become that animal. In your imagination enter its physical sensations. Your powerful muscles have been active earlier in the day. Now you have chosen to rest in a quiet, comfortable place. Feel the weight of your limbs as you let them completely flop. You are heavy, you are supported, you are safe. Feel your stomach and sides gently expanding and contracting with your breath. You are at peace. At this moment there is nothing for you to do, nowhere for you to go. You simply are.

✿ When it is time to move again, return to yourself and take a last look at your animal.

✿ Come to as an animal would—open your eyes, stretch, move your hands and feet, yawn if you feel like it, and get up slowly, feeling your feet on the ground.

Other
scenarios

You can create any scenario you like as an inspiration for your relaxation session, based on your own experience. There may be a place where you have felt especially at peace, like a favorite country walk, or a garden you have particularly enjoyed strolling round. Take yourself there in your imagination and repeat the experience. Feel the physical sensations of the experience as well as re-creating its image. Recall the weather—was it a warm, mellow, summer's day, or a crisp, cold, winter's day? Feel the grass beneath your feet, or the crunchy gravel of a garden path. Remember the scents of flowers and trees, and the sounds of birdsong and humming bees.

When you have finished, always allow a few moments to ensure that you are fully back to earth in mind and body. With practice, you will be able to recall the scene at any time to relieve tension and bring an instant feeling of relaxation.

Meditation

Many people take up meditation in order to relax and unwind, and although relaxation is necessary for meditation, the two are not the same. Meditation is a vast subject, including many different techniques and philosophies, and only a broad outline is given here.

The original aim of meditation is spiritual development; in most spiritual traditions it is a way of freeing the mind of everyday thinking, so that it becomes calm, clear, and receptive to entering a state beyond the everyday, in union with a higher consciousness.

A more immediate goal of meditation is to completely rest the body and the mind. It can be carried out lying or sitting, and will be accompanied by a comfortable feeling of looseness, and perhaps floating sensations in the body.

Meditation requires the spine to be upright, either in the classic cross-legged yoga position, kneeling with a support, or—more comfortably for many Westerners—sitting in a chair. Techniques for keeping the mind focused on the meditation can involve repeating a phrase or sound, chanting, visualizing a spiritual being like Christ or the Buddha, or simply being aware of one's breathing.

The brainwaves during deep meditation include not only some alpha and some theta, but also possibly some delta, which is the frequency of the brain during deep sleep. During deep meditation you may enter a delta brainwave state, but will also be awake and aware.

Meditation is best learned from a good teacher, but here is a simple form you may like to try, based on following the breath.

CIRCULAR BREATH MEDITATION

✿ Sit comfortably in a chair that supports your back. Make sure that the chair is the right height for you to have your legs uncrossed and your feet flat on the floor. Have your hands in your lap, palms upward. Close your eyes and relax. When you feel relaxed, start to focus on the sound of your breath as you breathe in and out. You may find it helpful to count as you take each breath in and out— go up to five, then return to one again.

✿ During the meditation, keep your breath to a natural rhythm, without forcing it. As you breathe in, imagine you are drawing in the breath from a point at the very base of your spine, up your spine to the top of your head. When you reach the crown of your head, begin to breathe out, imagining the breath coming down the front of your body, back to the point at which you started.

✿ Practice this circular breathing for up to 10 minutes, focusing your awareness on the breath all the time. You will probably find thoughts entering your mind; don't pursue them, simply let them go and turn your attention back to the breath.

✿ You should find this very calming, and you can practice this exercise at any time during the day, wherever you are, if you feel tense or stressed. When your time is up, come back to the world slowly. Stand up, stretch, and feel your feet on the ground before going into your next activity.

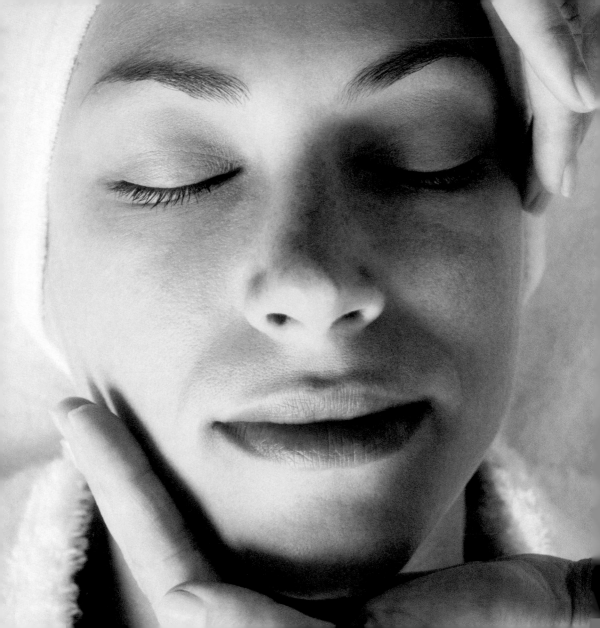

Beating pain

Everyone has aches and pains from time to time; some unfortunate people suffer all the time. Pain is the body's warning system, a way of telling us something is wrong and asking us to do something about it. The difficulty with ongoing, long-term pain, whether from injury, arthritis, or some other problem, is that although the situation is not an acute emergency, the brain continues to send out pain signals.

One response may be to try to suppress it with painkillers, and most people tend to tense up against the discomfort, which actually exacerbates pain by creating tight muscles and restricting the blood supply to the site. Sometimes we feel angry and rejecting towards the recalcitrant part of the body concerned, with the result that we withdraw energy from that part, giving it less of a chance to heal.

Techniques
for pain relief

If you have ongoing pain, you may find it hard to relax because you fear that the very act of lying still will bring the pain to the forefront. In fact, relaxation can help you come to terms with pain, and often relieves it. By learning to relax into the pain, you will stop resisting it and give the muscles and cells holding it there a chance to release. "Acceptance IS relaxation," writes the late Ursula Fleming, who taught pain control to cancer patients through simple relaxation.

I find it helpful simply to relax deeply, perhaps with some peaceful music in the background, noticing the pain without fighting it. Even if it does not completely remove severe pain, a relaxation session can still induce overall feelings of well-being, more relaxed muscles, and a better ability to cope. The important thing is to stop resisting so that your natural energy can flow through the body. On the following pages are some techniques that can help you to do this.

TECHNIQUE 1: **BREATHING INTO THE PAIN**

❀ Lie down to relax as described earlier, making sure that your body is as comfortable as possible. If it helps, support the painful area with a cushion.

❀ Now, focus on breathing in and out slowly and naturally, and when you feel relaxed take your awareness consciously to the painful area of the body.

❀ Instead of struggling against the pain or trying to resist it, simply accept and recognize the pain, and breathe into it.

❀ As you breathe out, imagine that your breath is gathering with it all the pain and tension, drawing them away to be released into the atmosphere where they can no longer harm you.

❀ Keep breathing healing energy into the area and breathing pain out for as long as is comfortable.

TECHNIQUE 2: **DRAWING ON THE LIFE FORCE**

❧ Lying down, fully relaxed, imagine healing life force entering your body with your breath entering your bloodstream and flowing toward the pain.

❧ Imagine it flowing lovingly around the painful area, soothing it, comforting it, and gently unknotting the tight muscles and blood vessels, allowing the blood to flow more freely.

❧ You may find it helpful in this exercise to introduce a color: blue and green, or a combination of both, are cooling and healing colors for pain. As you breathe in, imagine the blue-green light flowing toward the pain, surrounding it. As you breathe out, imagine the life force carrying all the pain and tension along your arms and legs, flowing out through your toes and fingertips.

❧ Continue for as long as is comfortable.

TECHNIQUE 3: **LOOKING AT THE PAIN**

❀ Lie down comfortably in the relaxation position, and take your attention to the painful area.

❀ This time, imagine what the pain looks like. You might see it as a red circle or blob, or some other image may come to you. What color is it? What shape is it? How big is it? Does it have any weight?

❀ As you continue to relax and watch the pain and pay attention to it, you may find it automatically changing color and shape; it may even start diminishing. You can help this process by visualizing the pain growing smaller and smaller, and eventually floating away like a bubble into the sky.

Everyone functions in their own way, and some people may find these suggestions more beneficial than others. If you find visualizing difficult, it is probably best to concentrate at first on the technique for breathing into the pain, which is a relatively simple visualization. When you have practiced this enough that you find it easy to imagine yourself breathing the pain away, you will be ready to try the other exercises. You may also be able to think of some techniques of your own—perhaps you might imagine the pain wafting away with a favorite piece of music, for example.

If you are suffering from severe, long-term pain, you may not get the instant results you will be hoping for—but do persevere, note the effects on your body and mind, and keep practicing.

You may also benefit from one of the bodywork therapies described on pages 109-121.

CHAPTER TWO
bodywork

> **66** *Relaxation helps us 'come home' to ourselves,*
> *it gives a feeling of coming back to our center.* **99**

Delcia McNeil

If you find it difficult to practice relaxation on your own, you are not unique. With today's frenetic pace of life, many people have forgotten the art of really being in touch with and listening to the body. Driven by ambition or by the necessity to work, people often override their physical and emotional needs, ignoring the pleas of their bodies' for rest, relaxation, comfort, and respect. Fortunately, there are now many helping hands available to bring us quite literally back to our senses. Many alternative and complementary therapies—those involving bodywork—are based on touch, and even if you don't have a specific health or pain problem, one or two sessions with a good therapist can be very valuable in reminding your body and brain what true, deep relaxation feels like.

The ideal way to find a good therapist is by personal recommendation, or through their professional register. Some medical doctors will recommend or even refer you to a therapist in preference to prescribing painkillers or tranquilizers. You can also find therapists in holistic health clinics, or advertised in your local health-food store or natural health pharmacy. Before you make an appointment, make sure the therapist is properly qualified and preferably listed on a professional register. A good therapist will tell you if they suspect that medical treatment is advisable.

There isn't space to describe all the bodywork therapies here, and some—such as osteopathy and chiropractic—are of course aimed at very specific health problems. But it is interesting to note that these therapies almost always induce relaxation in the patient. Apart from the specific techniques involved, the right touch given by a caring and skilled practitioner can have a powerfully healing effect.

Delcia McNeil, a healer, massage practitioner, and psychotherapist, says "It is my belief that when the body is in a deeply relaxed state the cells of the body are in an optimum state for regeneration." In addition, these therapies quite often lead to emotional healing. "The large majority of bodywork therapies involve relaxation as a key aspect of the treatment. The effect of this relaxation is to help the body to connect with trauma or tension that the person may not be conscious of and, depending on the form of bodywork, often a very gentle release can come. The relaxation induced provides a safe place in which the tension and sometimes memory of trauma held within the body's cells and muscles can be gently released."

People who have been unable to express grief, sorrow, and other painful emotions may find them surfacing during a session with a compassionate therapist, and be able to let go of them without being overwhelmed by them.

The therapies described here are some of the most popular and suitable for gaining the experience of deep relaxation. A complete guide is given in Delcia McNeil's *Bodywork Therapies for Women*.

case study
overcoming the symptoms of stress

The problem with ignoring the body's messages is that the body has a way of shouting more and more loudly until it forces us to listen. This was the case with Finnish-born Tanja, whose life came to a total standstill while she was still in her 20s. She told me her story.

"A few years ago I had a kind of crisis with migraines. I was getting them four or five times a week, the really severe kind where you can't do anything except lie down in a darkened room. I tried for a bit to carry on with medication, but it either didn't quite work or made me feel sick. I ended up in hospital and had to stop everything.

"I decided that I was really going to try and work through it, and reduce the stress that was causing it. At the time I was trying to get into documentary film production and I'd just got a job as a general assistant. I'd also just moved house, and I was having problems with my family. So all the nice ingredients were there! The migraines forced me to stop work completely and try and rebuild everything.

"When I was a child my father, a doctor, taught us a relaxation exercise: lying down and relaxing from the toes up, breathing, and feeling heavy, talking yourself into it. So the first thing I did was to start scheduling that into my life. I found that the more stressed I felt, the less I wanted to do the exercise. I think it's because when you are stressed, you are in the state of fight or flight, and the last thing you want to do is to let go of that—you feel you need it somehow!

"Then I went to a reflexologist, which I found very useful, because reflexology makes you relax! You discover how nice relaxing is, and then you can go home with the incentive to keep practicing.

"I'm doing Tae Kwon Do at the moment, which is not particularly relaxing—it's one of the martial arts—but I come away from that feeling very good. And you're getting rid of stress—as well as the physical movements, you shout out loud, you really let it all out!

"I also go to a yoga class. I do it a lot for the flexibility and physical benefits, but I very much like knowing that during that hour and a half class, that's all I think about. That's a very good way to let go.

"I've had very few migraines since coming back from that brink about five years ago—maybe two a year. That experience made me do a lot of thinking about how I was living my life and my mental approach. At that time I was driving myself too hard.

"When I eventually went back to work, I decided never to give work 100%, I'd stop at 80%. I had to do some terrible grappling with myself to come to that decision. I told myself no, no, no! If I'm doing a job I like I want to give it 100%. In the end I had to say, 'Listen Tanja, your 80% is going to be as good as some people's 100%, and that's all you're giving it.' It is a general principle I try and stick with, and I very much try to avoid putting in long hours.

"The migraine crisis made me aware that I can't do everything. I don't have as much energy as the people around me, and trying to act like them pushed me on—I didn't realize that I couldn't keep up, and was getting exhausted. These kinds of afflictions come from the personality, because you drive yourself to do so much. Now, though, I find that relaxation helps me a lot."

Like Tanja, quite young people today can suffer from severe stress symptoms. Whatever your age, building relaxation into your life is not a luxury but a part of good health care and prevention. And if you need a helping hand to learn to relax, it is easy to find one.

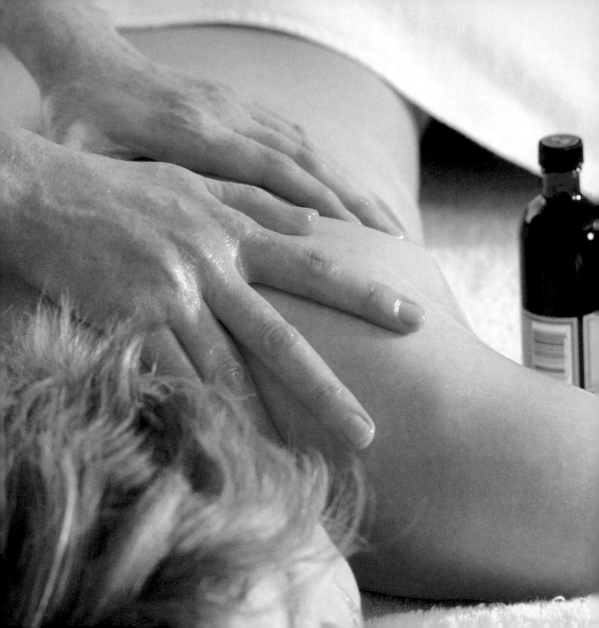

Massage

In the West the public image of massage has undergone a radical change in the last decade or so. Formerly, it was largely associated with the sex industry. Today more and more busy people are recognizing that touch doesn't have to be sexual, but that it can provide an enjoyable way to unwind. Massage has in fact more wide-reaching effects on the body and mind than just relaxation. Physically it can release chronic muscular tension, improve the circulation of blood and lymph, and relieve pain and arthritic symptoms, and it is very helpful for maintaining muscular tone in people who are bedridden or wheelchair bound. It can also clear the mind, relieve depression and restore a sense of wholeness and self-esteem by allowing the recipient to feel nurtured and cared-for.

Baby massage

Massaging one's baby or infant is a widespread custom in many parts of the world, but only recently has the value of massage been rediscovered in the West. It is an excellent method of relaxing both parent and child and for deepening the bond between them, and it is helpful in calming the child if it is unwell or suffering the pain of teething. It can also help to improve the baby's sleep patterns, especially if a soothing aromatherapy oil, such as lavender, is applied. It goes without saying that it will give the child comfort and help it to understand that it is loved and cared for. It may also help children to grow up to be in tune with their bodies, and to appreciate the importance of relaxation to their health and well-being. An acupuncturist tells me that her Indian patients who have received massage as infants have a more instant and aware response to her treatment, as if their nervous systems are wider awake.

Aromatherapy massage

Massage with aromatherapy oils is a very pleasant way to experience relaxation. Essential oils—distilled from flowers and other plants—take effect both by absorption through the skin and by reaching the nervous system through the nose and airways—hence they can be effective in a bath or in a vaporizer.

Each oil has several properties—lavender, for example, is sedative, antiseptic, and good for burns. A number of them induce relaxation—aromatherapist Robert Tisserand has found that inhaling tranquilizing oils, such as camomile, neroli, and bergamot, alters the pattern of the brainwaves, inducing calmness and a sense of well-being.

Because these deliciously scented oils are also very powerful, it is a good idea to go to a qualified aromatherapist who will ask you about any specific health problems before deciding on the right combination for you. For self-help with aromatherapy oils, see pages 208-211.

A back massage with a friend

Giving a massage can be almost as relaxing as receiving one, and you may like to exchange a massage with a friend or partner. However, don't give a massage after a heavy meal, or if your massage partner has a temperature or a serious skin, joint, or muscle condition.

Unless you own a massage table, the massage is best carried out on the floor, on a mattress or futon, covered with a large bathsheet. Make sure that you are comfortable too—not twisting or bending your back—and that you can use your bodyweight as well as your arms. If your partner is on the floor, kneeling is the best position.

Make sure the room is warm, turn down the lights, and put on some gentle background music to help create a relaxing atmosphere. As you work, be respectful of the other person's space. Keep conversation down, apart from asking your partner for feedback. Otherwise, allow them to relax mentally as well as physically.

You can buy a ready-mixed oil, or make up your own aromatherapy mixture using just a few drops of essential oil in a good carrier oil, or simply use talcum powder. Make sure that your hands are warm, and don't put cold oil directly on your partner's skin; pour a little into your palms at a time. Have another large bathsheet available to cover over the parts of your partner you are not working on.

Try starting with the back only if you are not experienced in massage, and remember to maintain a contact with your partner's body. Quite a number of techniques can be used, but for a first-time massage, it is probably enough to use stroking movements (up and down or circular), kneading, and 'hacking' for tight areas—using the sides of alternate hands in a fast chopping motion, to stimulate the blood and help relax knotted muscles. Your touch can be reasonably firm—check with your partner if the level of pressure feels good.

Begin by stroking the neck and shoulders in a smooth movement, then work your way from the shoulders down the arms, hands, and fingers. Then return to the neck and shoulders, kneading the area at the top of the shoulders. Gently massage any "ouch" spots for a little longer, using your finger pads in small circles. Follow this with a circular stroking around the shoulder blades, repeated several times. Then stroke your hands down the sides of the back to the base of the spine, and work your way back up either side of the spine using both hands, pressing with your thumbs. You can do this several times.

Complete the massage by brushing down your partner's spine several times with both hands. If he or she is very relaxed, allow them time to go on relaxing, or possibly snoozing.

It is best to receive your return massage on a separate occasion, so that you maintain your roles of giver and receiver.

A foot
massage

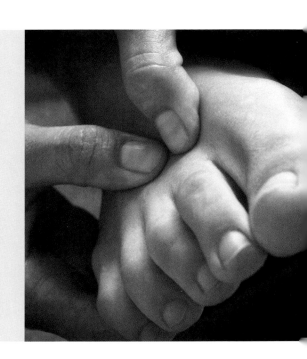

Having one's feet massaged can be incredibly relaxing, and again is something you can agree to exchange with a friend on a regular basis.

For this, your partner can lie down on a bed or sofa, if you can approach their feet comfortably and without twisting your spine—you should always be comfortable yourself. Use massage oil, talcum powder, or a foot lotion.

Start by holding both your partner's feet in your hands, to make contact. Then focus on one, completing this before turning to the other. Hold the foot in one hand, using the other hand for the massage. Begin by massaging in a circular movement in the hollow under the anklebones and then stroke over the instep, and under the heel. Next, enclose the foot in your whole hand, drawing your fingers and thumb down the front and sole of the foot simultaneously. Repeat this whole-foot stroking several times. Stroke down the bony side of the foot toward the big toe, and then cover this area again using small circular movements with the pads of your fingers.

Use your thumbs to apply gentle pressure to the area between the bones, pressing and releasing toward the toes. Again, use your thumbs to gently press and relax all over the sole of the foot. Use both hands to flex the foot and gently rotate the ankle.

Use the above guidelines—and also use your intuition about the kind of touch to use, and where to use it. Keep your touch fairly firm, though, especially if your partner is ticklish!

By the time you have finished both feet, your partner should be feeling beautifully relaxed. Gently squeeze each foot with both your hands in a finishing-off gesture.

Finally, always wash your hands thoroughly after giving a foot massage, as the feet can hold a lot of negative energy.

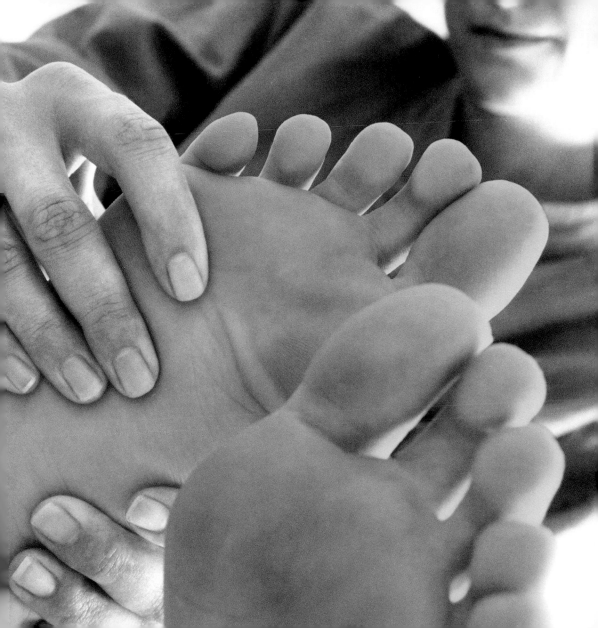

Alternative therapies

There are a number of ancient—and some not so ancient—therapies that are now being used to great effect as alternatives to conventional treatments. Many of these are based on the concept of balancing the energies within the body and harmonizing body and spirit to bring about good health and well-being. The ancient Chinese treatment of acupuncture works on this theory, as does the Japanese treatment of Shiatsu, and reflexology, a foot massage treatment known in Ancient Egypt. "Hands-on healing" is based on the idea of a spiritual energy being channeled through a healer to bring about self-healing.

An exception to this is the relatively modern treatment known as the Alexander Technique, which is based on learning a different, more relaxed way of holding the body.

Acupuncture

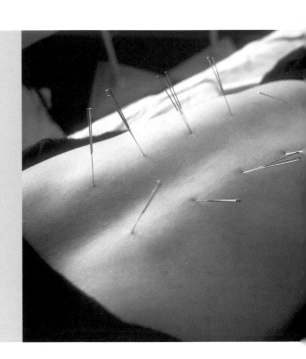

Having needles stuck into you may not sound particularly relaxing, but acupuncture is not necessarily painful (the needles are very fine) and it can be very effective in treating stress-related problems.

The theory of this ancient Chinese treatment is that the correct use of needles at specific points on the body (acupuncture points) can stimulate or sedate channels of energy called meridians, each relating to specific organs, emotions, and bodily systems. Scientific research has shown that acupuncture can trigger the production of endorphins, sometimes called "the body's own morphine," which have the effect of relieving pain and lifting the spirits.

Acupuncture has caught on widely in the West in recent years, and is now practiced by some doctors for pain relief; but it is perhaps best known as an aid to giving up smoking and other addictions. It can also be used to treat a wide range of physical and emotional problems.

Craniosacral therapy

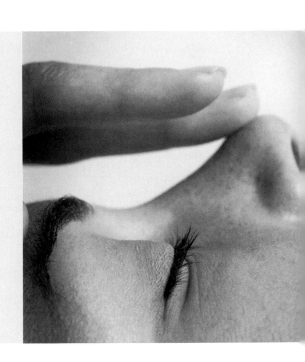

Craniosacral therapy developed out of a branch of osteopathy based on the discovery that the bones of the cranium (skull) are movable, and that the cerebrospinal fluid, which surrounds and nourishes the brain and spinal cord, fluctuates in a pulse-like rhythm. When there is disharmony in the body, this pulse does not fluctuate as it should.

Craniosacral therapy is used to relieve medical problems such as back pain, headaches, jaw problems, insomnia, tinnitus, and digestive disorders, and to release trauma from the body following an accident or injury. The treatment is light and noninvasive, and during the treatment one may enter a very relaxed, pleasant and dreamy state. It is so gentle that it is also very helpful for children, who rapidly relax under the therapist's touch. It has been used to great effect with problems of head banging, sleeplessness, and aggressive behavior, as well as chronic ear infections and postural problems.

Shiatsu

Developed in Japan in the 19th century, Shiatsu (which means finger pressure) is a form of massage using the oriental system of energy channels, or meridians. The aim, as in acupuncture, is to diagnose and treat imbalances in the body's energy system, using a range of techniques—not only finger pressure, but pressure with the thumbs, palms, elbows, and, occasionally, the feet. Treatment takes place with the client lying on the floor, fully dressed.

Shiatsu is effective for many chronic conditions such as back problems, sciatica, arthritis, migraines, asthma, constipation, and painful periods. It is excellent for improving the circulation both of the bodily fluids and of energy, and helping to define muscular tone. It can sometimes be painful, but the overall effect of a treatment is to relax and energize the body. Some people use it as a general tone-up, and as a means of unwinding.

Reflexology

Another very ancient technique (believed to have been practiced in Ancient Egypt), reflexology is based on the theory that all our bodily systems—bones, muscles, organs, and so on—are reflected and mapped out on the soles of our feet. Any areas of the feet that correspond to a problem area of the body will feel tender or painful when pressed by the reflexologist.

The technique of applying pressure in a specific way is believed to release energy blockages in the related organ or part of the body, and any pain experienced during reflexology will diminish as harmony is restored. Reflexology has been shown to be particularly effective with menstrual, fertility, and pregnancy problems, and postnatal symptoms, and nowadays it is often used to relieve pain in labor.

It is also a good treatment for insomnia and, as we saw in Tanja's story on pages 90-93, it has the effect of making you relax.

Hands-on
healing

Bringing about healing within the body by the apparently simple method of laying-on of hands is becoming increasingly acceptable today. This still mysterious means of transferring healing energy from one person to another comes under many names: spiritual healing, psychic healing, bio-energy healing, etheric healing, faith healing, and so on. I prefer to use the more general term "hands-on healing" to avoid the misguided and misleading connotations of spiritualism, magic, and miracle cures that once led this form of treatment to be viewed with suspicion.

However it may come about, it does seem that this form of healing is to some, a natural human ability. Many practitioners of other therapies are discovering, while they are in the process of applying the more formalized techniques to their clients, that they have healing hands as well.

Healers believe that they are drawing on, or "channeling," a universal spiritual energy that is not their own. By laying their hands on or near the client, this energy is transferred to the client's energy system, triggering their own self-healing mechanisms. Relaxation is one of the most immediate effects of this, possibly because the client stops fighting against the pain.

Healers sense and work with the system of subtle energy that interpenetrates and surrounds the body. Some work in their client's energy field (known as the "aura") without actually touching the body; interestingly, the client—lying with eyes closed on a massage table— may feel as if they are being touched physically when the healer's hands are actually a few inches away. Other pleasant sensations may be felt during a healing session, such as warm or sometimes cool currents flowing around areas of pain.

Healing is excellent in the treatment of stress and stress-related problems, and can be very effective at relieving pain. Many people respond positively to the human touch—even a reassuring squeeze of the arm can be helpful. Instant miracles are of course rare and should not be expected, but there is no doubt that healing can make a powerful contribution to a patient's cure.

As with other alternative treatments, healers aim to treat not only the body but also the emotions and spirit of the recipient, and the overall effects of healing can include a sense of positivity and feeling uplifted, as well as experiencing pain relief and relaxation. Sometimes one of the effects of healing is a release of emotional pain, and many healers will give their clients counseling as they are working, but it can happen that mental and emotional problems are lifted or clarified without a word being spoken.

case study an experience of healing

Janet, an actress in her forties, decided to try healing when she was going through a very fraught period in her life. The relaxation and sensations induced by the healing enabled her to get in touch with and acknowledge her deep-rooted feelings, and heal those too. This is her experience.

"This was the first time I'd had healing of this kind although I've always been interested in complementary therapies, and have used a number of different ones. I had become extremely stressed, anxious, and upset about a family crisis. I couldn't sleep properly, couldn't stop thinking and worrying about the problem. I was lucky enough to find Teresa through recommendation, and was reassured by the fact that she had professional qualifications both in psychology and healing.

But what impressed me most was her warmth and sense of humor, and what she told me about her personal experience of sacrifice and struggle to become a healer.

"She came to my home, and it was very relaxed and informal. I liked the fact that Teresa was happy for my cats to stay in the room, which felt very comforting. We began with a chat about my state of health and current circumstances. Then, because I was so stressed, we chose some ambient music to play in the background while Teresa gave me healing.

"I sat in a chair and she started by placing her hands around my head in my energy field, or aura, as she called it. It felt like I was being wrapped in a soft blanket. It felt rich blue in color, very warm and energizing. She placed her hands around but not on those parts of my body where I was suffering from a flare-up of psoriasis.

"I was very surprised at what happened during the session. It began by my becoming angry about the situation I was in, and I realized that I'd been angry with my family since childhood, but had never realized it before. I've always had difficulty in getting angry. Teresa explained this might be at the root of my psoriasis (which runs in the family).

"After I'd expressed my anger I became very still and had a sort of intuitive feeling that I must forgive the people I was angry with. I really didn't want to do this! What I wanted was revenge, to hurt them as I felt they had hurt me. I also didn't know how to forgive. So Teresa encouraged me to hold an imaginary conversation with them in my head. During this I realized that revenge was very petty and small, whereas forgiveness felt big, warm, and powerful. I was really, really tired of being small-minded. Somehow this changed something and I started to feel very peaceful.

"When Teresa's hands moved down to my chest, I felt a sharp pain by my left breast. She told me this was to do with my heart energy, which was where I was most stressed. She got me to take a deep breath and go with it, and as I did that, the pain went.

"She moved slowly down my body, and I could feel warm energy coming from her hands. While she was holding my feet she had an intuition about my diet and told me that visualizing a healthy body would help me. I knew I needed to look at my lifestyle, I'd neglected it badly during the crisis. When we'd finished I realized that not only did I feel better but I had also gained some insights into what had happened in the family and my childhood.

"Afterward, I felt wonderful—unburdened and relaxed. I decided that I needed to do this on a regular basis. It feels easier for me to switch off my thoughts and let go when someone else is guiding me."

Reiki

Reiki (a Japanese word meaning "universal life-force energy") is in many respects similar to hands-on healing. It is becoming increasingly widespread, probably because you can learn to start practicing it in a single weekend, and learn more techniques in further weekends. The ability to give out healing energy is passed on through initiation by a Reiki master, or teacher, using a set of ancient Buddhist symbols, and once transferred the recipient is able to give it to others. Reiki initiates are also encouraged to give themselves a daily treatment to keep their bodies and emotions in harmonious balance.

A Reiki treatment is more structured than hands-on healing. The client lies on a massage table and the therapist places his or her hands on a series of places on the body in a set order, sensing areas where the aura is damaged. The client can talk to the therapist or receive the treatment in total silence, depending on how he or she reacts.

The effects are very similar to those of hands-on healing, and can be equally gentle or powerful. One young woman who had been going through a difficult patch was advised to go to a Reiki therapist. A few months later she felt much happier and more in harmony with herself and the world, and commented that the treatments had made her more aware of her spiritual self.

A word of caution, however. Some Reiki masters ensure that their initiates undergo follow-up training and supervision. But because Reiki can be learned so quickly and practiced by anyone, not all those who practice it have been through the process of training and self-development now encouraged by long-standing healing bodies, nor are they all governed by similar ethical codes, or even aware of them. It is therefore advisable to go to a Reiki therapist whom you know something about or who has been recommended to you.

The Alexander Technique

The Alexander Technique is not a therapy in the sense of setting out to cure specific problems, but many conditions can be resolved through its practice—in particular stress and stress-related disorders, fatigue, insomnia, anxiety, neck and back pain, and digestive disorders. It is a way of learning how to use your body more easily and efficiently. It is a gentle, painless, physical process, taught on a one-to-one basis by trained teachers. It is an excellent way to learn to listen to your body, and it can improve your whole approach to life.

It was formulated nearly a hundred years ago by Frederick Matthias Alexander, an Australian actor who specialized in one-man shows. He was plagued by recurring problems of hoarseness and breathing difficulties, and found himself frequently losing his voice in mid-performance. Specialists found nothing physically wrong with him, however, and could only prescribe rest.

Alexander decided that since there was nothing wrong with his throat, the problem must lie in the way he was using it. He studied himself speaking in front of mirrors and realized that his voice was affected by the way he held his head and neck. He discovered that when he began to speak on stage he tended to contract muscles in his head and neck, and these in turn were related to tensions in the rest of his body. Over several years he taught himself new habits of movement, not only solving his voice problem but discovering new mental power and energy.

He started to teach his methods to others; his fame and popularity grew and in 1930 he began offering a three-year course for teachers. The Alexander Technique is now taught in countries all over the world.

The technique is particularly popular among performers and musicians—people whose bodies are important to them. A few years ago George, an orchestral musician, was in so much pain that he was about to give up his career. "By chance," he told me, "I was just coming to this decision when I got chatting with a fellow member of the orchestra who turned out to be an Alexander teacher. I started lessons with him and by the time I'd had four lessons all that pain had gone and I had decided to become an Alexander teacher myself."

The muscular pain that George was suffering was the result of what Alexander teachers call misuse of the body—something most of us suffer from to some degree. Most small children use their bodies easily and unselfconsciously, with perfect balance. By the time we become adults, however, the majority of us have acquired habits of moving, standing, and sitting that put unnecessary strains on the system. The results are muscular tension, bad posture and breathing, fatigue, and often back pain. In the case of musicians and sports people, this is often exacerbated by holding instruments awkwardly, or using one side of the body more than another.

The Alexander Technique aims to help you recover your natural ease and grace. This coordination of the body in all its movements is brought about by the teacher physically showing your body how it should be while standing, sitting, lying, and walking.

Lessons last 30–40 minutes, and it is essential to go to a qualified teacher. During the lesson the teacher places his or her hands on your body, guiding it gently to a better way of being, and showing you how to unlearn bad habits of posture and movement and to recognize and adopt a way of moving that is relaxed, and without tension or strain.

Janet, a drama student, was amazed by her first lesson. "My teacher touched me very lightly and told me to do nothing at all. Yet at the end I felt totally different—lighter and freer!" The technique is adjusted to each individual's needs and is largely nonverbal. Janet's teacher told her that his hands were "talking to her body." He did, however, tell her to think in terms of "directions" to her body as he moved it about, such as telling her neck to be free and her back to lengthen and widen, without actually trying to make these changes happen. After a while these directions become second nature.

The Alexander Technique can also be helpful with specific problems like back pain. When Elizabeth was 22 she hurt her lower back in a fall. Nothing was damaged; it ached a bit, but she didn't think much about it. "Suddenly, when I was on holiday, it got really painful—I could hardly move. The doctor sent me for X-rays but nothing showed up. They sent me to physiotherapy, where I was held up as an example of terrible posture—it was really humiliating. They gave me some exercises but they didn't help much, so I gave up.

"When I heard about the Alexander Technique, it sounded just what I needed. After a few lessons my backache began to improve. It occasionally comes back when I've overdone it; lying on the floor the way they show you really helps then. It also calms me down generally—in fact I feel calmer all round. A side effect of the technique has been to improve my breathing mechanism, and I'm getting over a slight stammer that I used to have when I got uptight."

Jane, a young mother of 23, finds it's changed her approach to housework. "I always used to be impatient to get things finished, living two jumps ahead of myself. These days I'm more conscious of what I'm doing, and I get much less tired. It's also made me realize the importance of touch. My teacher touches me so gently, yet it's very effective. I'm much more aware now of how I handle my little boy—I wince when I think of how I used to haul him around."

Alexander is helpful for children of 12 upward, when they can consciously participate. It can be very good for teenagers at a time when they are becoming self-conscious about their bodies or stressed by impending exams.

One of the technique's greatest benefits is a sense of being in harmony with oneself. As physical tensions melt away, mental attitudes may become more relaxed and people can often deal better with everyday problems. Andrea, a secretary in her 20s, says, "Not only do I get much less tired when I'm typing, but I operate much less automatically all round. I used to dive into work and get in a muddle, and when my boss snapped at me I'd snap back! Now, before starting a job, I think, "Hey, what's involved here?" And I'm less affected by my boss's moods. In fact, since I've been taking Alexander lessons, he seems to have got better tempered!"

LYING DOWN ALEXANDER STYLE

Students of the Alexander Technique are encouraged to lie down for 10–20 minutes twice a day, as described below. Lying in this position is excellent for the spine. One of its benefits is that during the activities of the day the disks between our vertebrae lose some of the fluid that helps them to act as cushions; this lying-down process restores the fluid to the disks.

❀ Place a telephone directory or large book under your head, so that your neck is at its normal angle to the body—neither thrown back nor thrust forward. Lie down and draw your knees up, with your feet flat on the floor shoulder-width apart, and your knees pointing toward the ceiling. Place your hands loosely on your abdomen.

❀ As you lie there, you will be letting your awareness go to your spine from head to toe. Feel your spine supported on the floor. Let your neck be soft and loose; let your facial muscles soften. Feel your shoulder blades on the floor. Think of your ribs widening and your chest opening out. Think of your back lengthening and widening. Think of your knees floating upward toward the ceiling. Let your breathing flow naturally.

❀ Occasionally people find their legs shaking; if this happens, don't try to control them, it is a sign of tension being released.

❀ As always, when you get up don't heave yourself forward: roll on to your side and then your knees, and get up slowly and gently using your hands and elbows to help you.

CHAPTER THREE

movement and exercise

> **66** *Every now and then go away,*
> *have a little relaxation, for when you*
> *come back to your work*
> *your judgment will be surer.* **99**
>
> Leonardo Da Vinci

The ideal way to experience really deep relaxation is to join a relaxation class, or to take up one of the oriental techniques that encourage harmony of mind and body, such as yoga, t'ai chi, or chi kung. These Eastern methods of movement take into account the existence of an energy system within and around the human body, and encourage the flow of subtle energy (prana in yoga, chi in the Chinese systems), which leads to a balance of mind, body, and spirit.

Although practicing relaxation on your own can be very beneficial, there is a lot to gain from joining a group run by an expert. Lots of busy people find it hard to give themselves permission to relax and let go. Being told to lie down on the floor and relax can get you over that hurdle. In addition, if you have any particular difficulties or questions a good teacher will be able to deal with them. It is also very supportive to be in a group of people all sharing the same aim, and possibly with similar problems. And of course, signing on and paying for a class gives you a degree of commitment to keeping it up.

Relaxation classes come in various styles, many involving movement. Look out for classes under headings like "Stress Management" as well as "Relaxation."

Autogenic Training

Autogenic Training consists of a series of mental exercises taught in groups or one-to-one over 8–10 weeks. "Autogenic" means "self-generating." It is a system that teaches you to enter a very deep state of relaxation, and can have the effect of altering your physical and psychological responses. It is said to increase efficiency and performance, whatever field you are in, from business to sport, creative writing to teaching.

It was first developed around 70 years ago by a German psychiatrist, Professor Johannes Schulz. Having studied yoga, hypnosis, and self-hypnosis, he realized just how much the mind can influence the body. He designed his series of exercises around 1932; later, one of his followers, Dr Wolfgang Luthe, set up training courses in

Montreal, after which Autogenic Training began to spread throughout the world. Numerous clinical trials have shown its effectiveness; for example, diabetics have been able to reduce their insulin intake as a result of the training.

Autogenic Training is usually taught in small groups; each weekly session lasts an hour and a half and you are asked to practice at home for 5–10 minutes three or four times a day, keeping a record of your experiences. During a session you sit or lie in a comfortable position and are taught to repeat to yourself a series of verbal statements suggesting relaxing bodily sensations. These include, for example, mentally repeating "My right arm is heavy," at the same time concentrating your thoughts on your right arm. Repeating these formulae induces a state of deep relaxation that allows the mind to calm itself by switching off the body's stress responses.

Over the weeks, new statements are added in, including suggestions of heaviness and warmth in the arms and legs, a calm regular heartbeat, easy natural breathing, and abdominal warmth. Other suggestions, such as a cool forehead, help to keep you alert. As you repeat these statements your body learns to respond to them, becoming relaxed but not too drowsy. Personal formulae— statements repeated in the relaxed state—may be added to help with specific goals in performance, motivation, or self-healing.

It is not advisable to try to learn Autogenic Training from books or tapes. Because of the deep effects on the nervous system, some people experience some physical or mental discomfort while taking the course, so it is essential that you are taught by a qualified instructor. (Autogenics trainers include qualified psychotherapists and doctors.) Sometimes emotional tensions or memories may bubble to the surface as a result of an increase in activity in the right side of the brain, which helps to release emotional blocks. This should not alarm you; on the contrary, releasing old emotional pains (something many of us resist) results in greater emotional balance and relaxation, and we free up the energy that was formerly used to bottle things up.

Vera Diamond of the British Autogenic Society, a psychotherapist as well as Autogenics instructor, told me, "It's never as bad as people fear! Part of the technique is called neutralization therapy, which neutralizes previous traumas by talking them through in the relaxed state. But you must work with a trained therapist.

"The basic Autogenic Training also includes 'Intentional Exercises' in which you verbalize feelings of anxiety. We teach people to cope with anger—we all need to cry and release that tension in a safe way on our own, and not over the wrong people at the wrong time as so often happens. So part of the aim of the basic course is to teach you to work with your own feelings."

Diane, 24, gave me this feedback after taking the course: "Initially my arms and legs felt very uncomfortable during some sessions, and all kinds of past memories came up, some quite painful, like the death of my father and a broken engagement. The instructor helped me to handle my feelings and to accept them when they surfaced. Afterward, those past events felt complete, and didn't trouble me any more. Now I feel much better about myself, and better able to handle my relationships."

Sally, a 30 year-old social worker, took an Autogenics course for stress prevention. She says, "Some of the people had health problems, and the results were quite dramatic. One young woman with irritable bowel syndrome was able to give up the medication she'd been taking for three years, a businessman cured his insomnia, and a couple of people got relief from backache. I had no health problems, but doing the training gave me more energy all round." It's also been found that several women with fertility problems have become pregnant after taking the course. (It is not uncommon for women to get pregnant once they relax.) Autogenics also helps people to give up smoking, tranquilizers, and other addictions.

A major benefit of Autogenic Training is that it alters the responses of your nervous system so that you automatically cope better with stressful situations. Vera Diamond explains: "With Autogenic Training you're switching from the fight-flight-freeze syndrome of the sympathetic nervous system to the parasympathetic nervous system whose function is rest-digest-recuperate. The intention is to switch automatically and easily from one to the other so that it becomes natural. It changes your stress chemistry, reducing the adrenaline surge. By letting go on a lot of levels you are gaining control at a deeper one. In a few weeks you can change so many patterns."

With stress at work becoming a widespread problem, it is good to know that some companies arrange Autogenic Training courses for their staff, with benefits both to individuals and the company. "We have discovered that people within companies work better together when they've done the training course together,' says Vera Diamond. "One company, with a very far-sighted Managing Director, got us to do two groups, with directors in one and senior management in the other. The following year the company won the prestigious Queen's Award for Industry."

Teachers, in a notably stressed profession, are turning to Autogenic Training, and there is a move to make it more available to children.

Autogenic Training for children

Children, sadly, are suffering more and more stress these days. Izzy Harrap, a dyslexia and dyspraxia therapist, was so enthused by the effects of Autogenics on herself that she now teaches it to children of 11 upward on a one-to-one basis. She finds that Autogenic Training is very beneficial with exam stress and helps children who have difficulty sleeping because of anxiety, either over exams or for other reasons.

She teaches them a shortened version of the course, usually lasting for five one-hour sessions. "It helps enormously because it balances up both sides of the brain—in children who are dyslexic and dyspraxic there are different areas of the brain that are not quite functioning at the same level. They are often so frustrated that they also suffer from behavioral difficulties, and the emotional-offloading exercises are pretty good for that—they are modified for children so that the process is very gentle."

Children with no specific learning difficulties can still get stressed by schoolwork, as can teenagers, many of whom suffer—some quite severely—from anxiety and insomnia brought on by pressure to achieve good results in exams. One teenage girl didn't have time to do the full course, and took only the first three sessions, but these were enough to help her sleep and as a result to feel calmer for her exams. Another of Izzy Harrap's students was a 12-year-old boy who had been not achieving at all well at school. Within a couple of months he was getting Merit awards. Izzy told me:

"I encourage them to do it at bedtime, and more often if they have the motivation, which the older ones often do. But they will all happily do it lying in bed. They get as much rest while doing the Autogenics as if they were sleeping. So it takes away the anxiety of thinking 'I've got to get off to sleep.'

"As they go to sleep they repeat their personal motivational formulae. I often introduce these quite early with children—it's very important to kids who have become used to thinking, 'I can't do it!' I ask them to choose their own statements to repeat to themselves. Lots of them pick 'I'm cool'; the boy who started getting Merit Awards chose, 'I'm brilliant, I'm at ease, and I can enjoy my school work.' It helps them to have a much more positive self-image. Children respond really well, and often find that things turn around for them very quickly."

Having a positive self-image is helpful not only with academic achievement, but also with the many other pressures associated with childhood and growing up in our modern age—fitting in with and being accepted by their peer group, for example, and accepting their physical appearance.

Yoga and Pilates

Yoga developed as part of the ancient Hindu religion, and may be 5,000 years old. The word yoga derives from a Sanskrit word meaning "union" and its original purpose was as part of a spiritual path aimed at enlightenment. In the West, however, taking up yoga does not mean that you have to adopt Hindu beliefs. It can be learned as a purely physical practice for people who want it for exercise and relaxation.

German-born Joseph Pilates was a sickly child who later took up sport to overcome physical weakness. During World War I he devised a fitness program, and after the war he moved to New York where top performers and athletes were drawn to the program, which "built strength without adding bulk, balancing that strength with flexibility and achieving the perfect harmony between mind and muscle."

Pilates

Pilates is very much concerned with relaxation in movement. It is a conditioning technique that can be learned in a studio using special types of equipment, with one-to-one guidance from a trained consultant. It can also be practiced as "floor-work" in a class, with no equipment, which is enjoyable and effective. Its aim is to tone and strengthen muscles using slow, controlled movements and stretches.

Pilates is a popular method of exercise and body maintenance among sportspeople, dancers, and other performers, as well as for sedentary people who want to keep fit. It is suitable for people with back problems and sports injuries, who are often referred to classes by physiotherapists or doctors. (If you do have a problem, check with your MD or consultant before embarking on a class.). Pilates is also excellent for older people who want to maintain fitness and flexibility without strain, or to combat the stiffening effects of arthritis.

The exercises are underpinned by eight basic principles:

❀ Concentration   ❀ Control

❀ Breathing   ❀ Flowing movement

❀ Placement   ❀ Relaxation

❀ Centering   ❀ Stamina

In a pilates class you will not experience the 20–30 minutes of pure relaxation that is common to most relaxation classes. You will, however, find that you learn to relax in action as you carry out each of the movements—every part of the body is systematically worked during the session.

As well as improving your figure (producing sleeker muscles, tighter tummies, and improved posture) the benefits include an increased awareness of how you use your body. No movement is made without correct postural alignment being taken into consideration. There is an emphasis on using both sides of the body equally (we all tend to favor one side more than the other, often without being aware of it, allowing the other side to become lazy and stiffen.)

Teachers will look out for places where you are holding stress or are out of balance and help you to correct those problems. As with the movements themselves, breathing is unforced, but deliberate: as a rule, you breathe in to prepare for a movement and breathe out while carrying it out.

During the hour you spend in a class you are entirely focused on the here and now, as you concentrate on each slow movement. Many of the exercises are carried out lying on the floor, and this can become quite meditative. People who have attended a pilates class to address a physical problem usually leave with a renewed sense of relaxation and well-being.

Yoga

Yoga has been found to have marked health benefits among those who practice it regularly. It is good for stress, insomnia, chronic fatigue, asthma, heart conditions, high blood pressure and circulatory disorders, back and neck pain, and bad posture. It is, however, contra-indicated for anyone with a serious back problem, particularly spinal injury, and not all the asanas are suitable for pregnancy. It is therefore important to go to a fully qualified and experienced teacher, and if you have a medical disorder you should check with your doctor first.

A number of different styles of yoga have been developed, some more strenuous than others. Hatha yoga—the type taught chiefly in the West—emphasizes the physical aspect. It includes asanas (postures) and pranayama (breathing exercises), both of which help to channel prana, the body's life energy. Most classes include a period of relaxation lying on the floor, which also encourages energy to flow.

"Yoga can be taught gently and purely for relaxation, or it can be taught for strength and flexibility, which will make you feel better in that way," says Renate Lalloo, who teaches yoga in London. "The nice thing is that the different styles attract different kinds of people. Depending on where you're at, there will be a way in yoga for you if you are willing to look around."

It's important to find a teacher who suits you. Eleanor, a hardworking designer who wanted to learn yoga for relaxation, tried one class which she found too strenuous for her needs. Then she found a teacher who taught a much gentler method, "which enabled me to keep my body moving, even when I was very tired. If you're busy, it's much better to do some gentle exercise than to sit and do nothing—it keeps your energy going. It also gives me a feeling of groundedness and well-being."

The Hindu tradition holds that we do not end at our physical selves, but are surrounded by a subtle energy body. Good health depends on the unimpeded flow of prana, which flows through the body via a multitude of energy channels called nadis—ill-health results when that flow is disturbed. A harmonious balance of prana is achieved through exercise, breathing, relaxation, diet, and meditation.

As well as the nadis, we have seven centers of energy, the chakras, which correspond to nerve centers and glands in the physical body; these receive and give out prana, and the energy in each needs to be in harmony with itself and with the others. The asanas are designed to work on specific chakras, energizing and clearing them. Physically, these postures systematically stretch and tone every part of the body, including the muscles, spine, and joints, loosening tight areas. They also massage the internal organs and glands.

"Working through your body has a positive effect on your breathing and on your mind," explains Renate Lalloo. "So relaxation of the mind is reached through working on the body."

Working on the whole being can enable people to become more fully themselves. Renate told me: "It has changed my own life completely! I used to work as a nurse and found it very stressful. Doing yoga gave me the courage and confidence to get out. My relationships have changed totally, because I am now moving among totally different kinds of people. It's opened a door to a whole new set of avenues, meeting people with a more spiritual approach to life.

"Probably the majority of people come to my classes for stress reduction and relaxation. They get it if they stick it out—not everyone is aware that yoga is actually quite hard work, not a wonder cure, and that they have to do something for themselves."

Yoga breathing

In yoga, breathing (pranayama) plays an important part, and the breath is synchronized with the movements. Breathing is always through the nostrils, and the emphasis is on breathing out: the more you exhale, the more stale air and toxins you are clearing from your body. The breath connects us to the nadis. The left nostril is connected to the Ida nadi, which is related to the cooling Moon energy; this controls the left side of the body and the right side of the brain—the intuitive, dreamy, and emotional side. The right nostril is connected to the Pingala nadi which is related to the warming Sun energy; this controls the right side of the body and the left side of the brain, which is the logical, rational side.

CALMING PRANAYAMA

This form of alternating breathing helps to bring the two sides of the brain into balance, producing calm and clarity. (You may feel like blowing your nose during this exercise, but this is quite natural; you may also feel a little dizzy at first, but this will lessen as you practice.)

❧ Seated in a chair, close your eyes, relax your body, and still your mind.

❧ Place your dominant hand around your nose. If you are right-handed, rest your right thumb against your right nostril, with your fingers lying toward your left nostril.

❧ Breathe in, then close the right nostril gently with your thumb and slowly exhale through the left nostril.

❧ Now inhale through the left nostril.

❧ Swap nostrils and exhale and inhale on the other side.

❧ Keep the breath smooth and relaxed, without trying to breathe in extra deeply.

❧ Alternate this breathing through the nostrils for about 5 minutes.

The chakras

The chakras are recognized by a number of metaphysical systems, as well as yoga. Many healers refer to them, and can sense their energy with their hands; a few can see them. Chakra is a Sanskrit word meaning "wheel" and these energy centers are perceived as whirling vortices of energy. There are seven main chakras, each located at both the back and the front of the spine, vibrating at increasing speeds as they move up the body. There are also a number of minor chakras, including the palms of the hands and the soles of the feet.

The function of the chakras is to take in and give out energy. They can become overactive, or depleted of energy, through physical and emotional stress, and the aim of any chakra-oriented therapy (like yoga or healing) is to restore balance and harmony to all of them.

The energy body, of which the chakras are an integral part, forms a link between the human being's physical, emotional, and spiritual selves. Each chakra relates to a particular part of the endocrine (glandular) system, and also to particular emotions and attitudes, and each has its own color. Although there are variations among different systems, the description given below is widely accepted.

ROOT OR BASE CHAKRA

COLOR
Red

LOCATION
Base of spine

GLAND/BODY PART
Adrenals, reproductive organs, legs, feet

MENTAL/EMOTIONAL ASPECTS
Physical energy, sense of security, groundedness, possessions and money

SACRAL CHAKRA

COLOR
Orange

LOCATION
Lower back

GLAND/BODY PART
Reproductive system, kidneys, bladder, abdomen, lower spine

MENTAL/EMOTIONAL ASPECTS
Sexuality, creativity, ability to act, relationships

SOLAR PLEXUS CHAKRA

COLOR
Yellow

LOCATION
Midback

GLAND/BODY PART
Liver, stomach, gall-bladder, diaphragm, pancreas, spleen

MENTAL/EMOTIONAL ASPECTS
Anger, resentment, hurt, sadness, fear

HEART CHAKRA

COLOR
Green

LOCATION
Center of chest

GLAND/BODY PART
Heart, lungs, circulation, breasts, ribcage, thymus

MENTAL/EMOTIONAL ASPECTS
Unconditional love, compassion, self-acceptance, giving and receiving

THROAT CHAKRA

COLOR
Sky blue

LOCATION
Hollow of throat, back

GLAND/BODY PART
Throat, neck, ears, voice

MENTAL/EMOTIONAL ASPECTS
Communication, self-expression, ability to listen, truthfulness

BROW CHAKRA

COLOR
Indigo

LOCATION
Center of brow ("the third eye")

GLAND/BODY PART
Brain, pituitary gland

MENTAL/EMOTIONAL ASPECTS
Rational and intuitive thought, intellect, idealism

CROWN CHAKRA

COLOR
Violet

LOCATION
Top of the head

GLAND/BODY PART
Cerebral cortex, cranium (skull), pineal gland

MENTAL/EMOTIONAL ASPECTS
Spirituality, extrasensory perception, higher thinking

A MEDITATION VISUALIZING THE CHAKRAS

For this meditation, you can lie down but you may find it preferable to sit in a chair, with your back supported and your feet flat on the ground. Have your hands loosely in your lap, palms upward.

If you don't find it easy to visualize, don't strain. Simply know that the chakras and their associated colors are there. Remember that they are located within your body at the back of your spine as well as the front.

✿ Take your attention to the area of your body around the bottom of the spine and lower abdomen. This is the location of the root chakra, which connects you with the earth. Imagine this chakra as a deep red flower, circling clockwise. Breathe into this area, breathing in red energy, and as you breathe out let go of any insecurities and anything that is not supporting you.

✿ Move up to the area of your abdomen about two inches below the navel, and imagine the sacral chakra, your center of creativity. Imagine it as an orange flower, circling clockwise. Breathe into this center, breathing in orange energy and creativity and breathing out any doubts or blocks to your creativity.

✿ Move up to the area of your diaphragm, and visualize your solar plexus chakra, the center of your self-worth, as a bright yellow flower, circling clockwise. Breathe into this center, breathing in yellow energy and courage, and breathing out any fears, doubts, anger or sadness.

✿ Move up to your heart center, which is in the middle of your chest. Visualize it as a green flower, circling clockwise. Breathe in brilliant green energy, at the same time breathing in love and compassion, and breathing out any sorrow or resentment.

❀ Move up to your throat center, at the base of your throat. Visualize it as a light blue flower, circling clockwise. Breathe blue light into this center, at the same time breathing in clarity and breathing out any fears you have in expressing yourself.

❀ Move up to your brow center, located between and just above your eyebrows. Visualize it as an indigo flower, its petals circling clockwise. Breathe in inspiration and clear thinking and breathe out any mental confusion or worries.

❀ Move up to your crown center, located at the very top of your head, and visualize it as a violet-petalled flower, circling clockwise. Breathe in violet light and with it breathe in your openness to your higher wisdom, breathing out any doubts or resistance.

❀ Now imagine a beam of white light above you, coming straight down through the crown center and through each of the chakras in turn, bathing each one in cleansing white light. Spend a few moments on this, and imagine that the white light is enclosing each of your chakras, so that they give out positive energy but are protected against any negative influences from outside.

✿ When you sense that all your chakras have been bathed in this white light, come gently back to reality. Open your eyes, and feel your feet firmly planted on the ground.

T'ai chi and chi kung

The slow, flowing, graceful movements of t'ai chi and chi kung are practiced by millions of people in the East for the health of mind and body. Although they are actually oriental martial arts, in China their benefits are medically recognized, and they form part of normal hospital therapy. Today they are growing in popularity in the West.

In ancient China, exercise was regarded as important for both mind and body. The Chinese philosophy of life understood everything as being in a potential state of movement and changing balance; man needed to be able to flow with the changes, at the same time keeping a sense of stability and balance. The Chinese developed a number of movement styles, including highly aggressive fighting techniques and others that are more quiet and meditative.

The ancient Taoist philosophy on which both t'ai chi and chi kung are based emphasizes living in tune with nature, paying attention to diet and health, and taking regular exercise to keep the body fit and youthful. Taoists see all creation, including ourselves and our environment, as being composed of an ever-changing blend of two opposite forces of energy, yin and yang. In general, yin represents femininity, darkness, water, and physicality, while yang represents masculinity, light, fire, and spirituality. Good health depends on a harmonious balance of yin and yang within your body, allowing chi, the life force, to flow freely. When chi flows freely, you feel a sense of harmony and well-being, but when it is obstructed—by stress, for example—ill-health results.

Both t'ai chi and chi kung work on the acupuncture meridians running through the body, through which chi flows. Certain movements and positions aim at clearing and balancing specific meridians. Breathing plays an important part; people who practice regularly find their breathing deepening and slowing down from its normal, often unnaturally shallow state.

Both systems can be practiced by people of any age—the Taoists believed that they helped to keep the body young as well as fit. Enhancing the body's subtle energy simultaneously enhances physical health, strengthening the immune system and the heart and circulation, and improving co-ordination and balance.

T'ai chi and chi kung are becoming increasingly popular in the West. Privately run classes are advertized in local newspapers, health stores, and libraries, and you may well be able to find a local class. Students are encouraged to practice daily, if possible; it is through regular practice that the real results are achieved.

By letting go on many levels you are gaining control at a deeper one.

case study
releasing tension through t'ai chi

Jenny, a 30 year-old school counsellor, says, "Before I started doing t'ai chi I was always rushing round trying to do six things at once, falling over my own feet, and getting stressed and exhausted. Now I seem to be able to go about things more calmly. I can concentrate more easily, and don't get so tensed up."

Elsa, another busy young career woman, had no idea how to relax or how to manage her free time. "I just couldn't cope. I got so tense I was afraid I might have a cardiac arrest! I knew I had to change something in my life. I'd already tried a Korean martial art called sul ki do, which is very tough. I'd strained my back and I found the techniques altogether too aggressive. Then I decided to learn t'ai chi instead. Around the same time I changed to a homeopathic doctor, who found I had gallstones and put me on a completely new diet, and this made me feel much healthier and more energetic. I also tried some deep massage treatment.

"It's difficult to say which aspect of all these changes helped me the most, but I'm sure t'ai chi has played a very important role. It enables me to relax into the moment. Even a few minutes' practice can unwind me and allow me to spend the next hour calmly. For example, I once had a rush job to complete in an hour: I spent five minutes doing t'ai chi in the bathroom, and that enabled me to spend the next hour calmly completing my project.

"I'm much more in tune with nature now. I can go out and do 20 minutes' practice in the park at lunchtime and when I go back to work I feel as if I've spent the whole day outside—it's wonderful."

Chi kung (also spelled qi gong) has many similarities with t'ai chi, including the slow, conscious, graceful movements. However, it is more static: most movements are carried out standing with the feet shoulder-width and parallel, and the knees slightly bent, while the body turns from the waist and hips. There are literally hundreds of different chi kung styles and movements. As with t'ai chi they have poetic-sounding names, like "Holding up the Sky," and "Crane Takes Water." The name chi kung means "energy work."

Some of the positions such as "Tree Meditation" and "Holding the Barrel" are held for increasing lengths of time (3–5 minutes for beginners.) Newcomers find this tough on the legs at first, but these standing postures encourage circulation in the legs and knees, and throughout the whole body. They are forms of standing meditation, and keen students may practice them for up to an hour at home!

CHI KUNG SLOW SWINGING EXERCISE

This is very calming. Practice it for a few minutes before lying down to relax, or when you feel stressed, or before you go to bed.

❖ Stand with your feet shoulder-width apart, and parallel (toes pointing forward), knees slightly bent.

❖ Hold your arms loosely by your sides, with a slight gap in your armpits, and the backs of your hands facing forward.

❖ Turn slowly to the right from the waist and hips, bending your right knee as your weight falls on it. Keep your shoulders and head level.

❖ Turn slowly back to the center, so that both knees are bent equally, and then turn smoothly on to the left, bending your left knee as your weight falls on it.

❖ You can do this with your eyes closed if you like. Keep the movement very slow and smooth, for 5–10 minutes.

Healing power

While practicing t'ai chi and, particularly, chi kung, students often become aware of the presence of their invisible chi and may experience buzzes of energy in different parts of their body, while healers find that the healing energy in the palms of their hands is enhanced. In fact there is a branch of chi kung that concentrates on developing this healing power, both for oneself and for others.

There have been many clinical trials carried out in China to identify the medical benefits of chi kung. It has been shown to be effective in improving heart function and blood pressure, digestive and respiratory problems, as well as benefiting cancer patients, alongside conventional treatments. Brainwave patterns also slow down, with an increase in alpha and theta waves, and greater coherence between the two halves of the brain.

Many classes start with a period of total relaxation lying on the floor, with the focus on abdominal breathing (the occasional snore is sometimes heard as students unwind). In the Chinese energy system there is an important energy center in the belly, the Tan Tien (or Dan Tian) which lies an inch below the navel (equivalent to the sacral chakra). Chi kung exercises build up the energy in this center so that it can be drawn on during the rest of the day.

One of the advantages of chi kung is that it is an ideal form of physical and relaxation exercise to be practiced by the elderly and the disabled; many of the movements can be carried out seated if necessary, and will bring a sense of achievement as well as harmony and well-being.

RELAXATION ROUTINE FOR BEGINNERS:

A RELAXATION USING THE MERIDIANS

In this relaxation you will be helping chi energy to flow through your meridians, healing and clearing your body of toxins and staleness.

There are 12 major meridians, six on each side, which correspond to organs and systems in the body. Don't strain to visualize them clearly or work out which is which, as tension or effort will block the flow. Simply be aware that these channels exist and trust the chi to do its work. Take your time over it, and enjoy it.

❁ Lie on the floor in your usual relaxation position, hands a little away from your sides, palms upward, and feet slightly apart.

❁ Be aware of your back where it touches the floor. Feel the floor supporting you. Allow your breathing to become calmer and deeper.

❁ Now imagine that you are breathing in chi through the sides of your head, down through the sides of your throat and neck and through your arms down to your fingertips. As you breathe in, let the energy enter your system, and as you breathe out let it travel down. Allow the pure clean chi to travel along your arms, clearing any blockages and stagnation. Sense any stale, stagnant energy leaving your body through the fingertips. Take your time, and have a sense of letting go.

✿ Next, breathe in through the whole of the front of your face. Breathe in the clean, energizing chi, and allow it to flow through and down the front of your body, inside and outside, ironing out any tensions, and bathing your internal organs. Take your time. Let the chi flow down the front of your legs, clearing any blockages and clearing and energizing the meridians. Imagine the energy running down through your thighs, knees, and ankles, relaxing your muscles and loosening the joints as it flows right down to the big toe. Let any stale or stagnant energy run out through your toes. Take your time, and let go.

✿ Now, imagine that you are breathing in through the back of your head, sending energy down the whole of your spine and back, through your hips and buttocks, and down through the backs of your knees, calves, and ankles to the soles of your feet. Allow the clean, energizing chi to relax and cleanse your whole system. Take your time and let go, as you allow any stale, unwanted energy to flow out through the soles of your feet.

✿ Now take a few minutes to enjoy the sense of your body lying on the floor, with the chi flowing through it, renewing your energy for your next activity.

✿ Get up slowly, as always, feel your feet on the floor. Stretch and yawn if you need to.

case study a new way of life

For Ilona Tate the discovery of t'ai chi and chi kung literally transformed her life. She told me:

"In my 20s I was not in good health at all, I was probably neurotic, and certainly quite highly strung. I had quite serious mood swings, lost my temper quite easily, and was generally quite anxious, and on a short fuse. I suffered from allergies, asthma, and eczema, was smoking 20–30 cigarettes a day, and drinking quite heavily as well! It really was a recipe for physical and mental disaster.

"I started t'ai chi and chi kung when I was 27. I had trained as an artist and illustrator, but at the time I was on benefits, very short of money, and constantly worried about getting through the week financially. I had got into quite a bad scene in terms of drugs and so on—it wasn't that I was doing much in the way of drugs myself, but the people I was involved with during that time were very unhealthy in terms of mind and body.

"I think when you take pot or things like that, you are looking for the same buzz that you get after the chi kung class—you are calm and relaxed, and everything's very vibrant! I think I took up chi kung because I wanted the same kind of feeling, but in a healthy way.

"Chi kung was recommended by a perceptive friend who recognized I needed a bit of help, and I joined a class at a local community center where they offered concessionary rates. I had tried doing meditation by myself, and found that I couldn't still my mind enough just sitting there—it was important for me to move. I've always been interested in dancing and gymnastics, so I was aware of the body-mind connection.

"After the first lesson I went to—which included both t'ai chi and chi kung—I felt absolutely fantastic. I could feel the chi in my hands, they were tingling, and I thought, "This is what I'm meant to do!"

"Gradually I started doing more and more chi kung. The benefits have become apparent over a number of years. I'm a lot calmer and a lot more sure of myself. Sometimes I shock people because I say what I feel, I like to be authentic, and just say what's in my heart, and what comes out is who I am. That feels really good.

"I have stopped smoking and drinking, and very rarely get ill now. It wasn't at all easy to stop smoking, but when I took over a regular class and started teaching the breathing techniques, I decided I wanted to do more work with breathing. I was still smoking on and off, but it just felt really foul to do an hour's chi kung, come out feeling calm and relaxed, and then put noxious fumes in my lungs afterward!

Even after I'd made the decision to stop, it was quite hard for three or four weeks, but practicing chi kung techniques helped me get through the craving."

Ilona now teaches both t'ai chi and chi kung. "They are different. I like doing t'ai chi because it's more complex, slightly more demanding on the body, and very good for building up muscular strength in the legs. And you tend to work more with other people, doing pair work. Chi kung is more a time of meditation, getting to know yourself, feeling comfortable internally with your own self and your energy. It's more quiet and calming.

"Another effect is what I think is called synchronicity. I find that if I have in my mind something I'd like that is healthy and beneficial, it seems to come along without any effort, and at just the right time. For example, if I've got a particular problem in my life and I need a solution, I might be in a bookshop and the right book will kind of make itself known to me. And my relationships have become really healthy and good.

"Another effect of doing it—you could call it spiritual—is that I've become more in touch with nature and the beauty of nature, and feel more connected with plants and animals and birds. I feel that I'm really part of nature, and I feel the richness and the beauty of it much more than I used to. And with that too comes forgiveness, and being kind and compassionate, and approaching situations with what Buddhists call loving kindness. I have a generosity of spirit which I did not have, without expecting anything in return. Instead of wondering whether I'll get anything back, I can trust in being able to give out without needing anything back. I find it comes back anyway, not necessarily how you expect it."

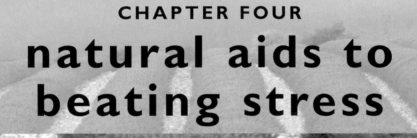

CHAPTER FOUR

natural aids to beating stress

> *66If you need medical advice,*
> *let these three things be your physicians;*
> *a cheerful mind, relaxation from business,*
> *and a moderate diet.99*

Schola Salern

If you have serious health problems, you are advised to seek help from a qualified therapist. But the field of natural and alternative therapies is also full of possibilities for self-help using natural means.

Aromatherapy has become very popular in recent years. The essential oils used are readily available and have a huge range of properties, covering both physical problems, and mental and emotional ones.

Flower remedies, derived from the essences of flowers and other plants, are a gentle way to promote a positive mental state. Crystals are beautiful to look at and each has individual properties to aid a number of mental and physical imbalances; and sound has an extraordinary ability to calm and relax the mind and body.

Herbal remedies and teas are a useful alternative to medication for minor complaints, although some precaution is necessary—always read the label and take advice if you are unsure. And perhaps the easiest and most natural way to make positive changes to our health and attitudes is through diet—a healthy eating plan, plenty of water, and vitamin supplements if necessary form a good basis for a relaxed mind, body, and spirit.

Aromatherapy oils

The best ways to use essential oils for aromatherapy at home are by inhalation, either in a vaporizer or in your bath, adding no more than 7–8 drops to the water. You can also add a drop or two to a bowl of pot-pourri, or put a few drops on a handkerchief or piece of cotton wool to sniff—but don't overdo it, they are very powerful.

You can use them for self-massage, but make sure they are well diluted in a carrier oil. Never use them undiluted on the skin; I once put a couple of drops of lavender oil directly on my pillow to help me sleep and woke in the morning with red bumps on my cheek!

A few drops in water in a vaporizer with a lighted nightlight beneath can fill your room with delicious scent and help to lift your spirits and relax you at the same time. You can use more than one oil at a time. Make sure you get good-quality oils; the cheaper ones are usually diluted. Keep the bottles out of reach of children.

For relaxing body and mind, the following oils are suitable. (Only their mental and emotional properties are listed here.)

CEDARWOOD
Calms anxiety and nervous tension.
Aids concentration and mental focus.
Good for meditation.

CAMOMILE
For the highly strung, and for people
who drive themselves hard.

CLARY SAGE
Good for nervous exhaustion, insomnia
from overwork, and headaches.
Relieves indigestion.

EUCALYPTUS
Cools heated emotions, and balances
mood swings. Antiviral, antiseptic, and
decongestant.

FRANKINCENSE
For mental fatigue, exhaustion,
depression, insecurity, and panic.
Aids meditation.

GERANIUM
Antidepressant. Good for panic and
acute anxiety. Balances mood swings.

LAVENDER
Excellent for all forms of anxiety and
tension, and for feelings of panic.

MARJORAM
Soothing and relaxing; good for
mental strain.

ORANGE
Excellent for depression, sadness,
and lack of joy. Lifts the spirits.

ROSEMARY
Clears headaches and mental fatigue.
Stimulates the memory.

SANDALWOOD
Helpful for worry about past and future;
brings peace and acceptance.

Flower
remedies

There are hundreds of remedies on the market derived from the essences of flowers and other plants. The best known are probably still the original Bach Flower Remedies, developed early in the last century by Dr Edward Bach, a physician and homeopath. After much research, Bach concluded that illnesses are caused by negative mental states which affect physical health. He spent many years searching the countryside for a solution in the plant kingdom, ultimately finding 38 plants whose vibrations can reharmonize negative mental states.

Bach Flower Remedies are quite safe to use, including for children. Up to six remedies can be combined: put two drops of each in spring water in a dropper bottle. Take four drops, further diluted in water, four times a day—or whenever you feel stressed. Rescue Remedy, a combination of five remedies, is an all-purpose remedy for shock, terror, panic, emotional upsets, stage fright, exam nerves, and so on.

These Bach Flower Remedies are for anxiety and tension.

ASPEN
For anxiety, apprehension, and fear of unknown things.

CHERRY PLUM
For fear of mental collapse and loss of control.

ELM
For temporary feelings of inadequacy, and being overwhelmed by responsibilities.

GORSE
For despair, hopelessness, and despondency.

HOLLY
For anger, jealousy, and vengefulness.

IMPATIENS
For impatience and irritability.

LARCH
For lack of self-confidence.

MIMULUS
Fear of known causes, shyness, and timidity.

OLIVE
For exhaustion and weariness, mental and physical.

RED CHESTNUT
For excessive fear or anxiety for others.

ROCK ROSE
For terror, extreme fear, or panic.

ROCK WATER
For those who are hard on themselves, workaholic, and self-denying.

STAR OF BETHLEHEM
For all kinds of shock, mental or physical.

WHITE CHESTNUT
For persistent unwanted thoughts, preoccupation with worry.

Prewedding nerves

Ginette had suffered from anxiety and panic attacks since the age of ten. When she became engaged, prewedding nerves brought on more panic attacks, in which her heart raced, she found it hard to breathe, and her throat closed up. Her doctor at first prescribed medication, which did not help. Fortunately, the doctor had recently discovered the Bach Remedies, and on her next visit he treated her with Rock Rose (for terror) and Mimulus (for fear of known causes). Within a month her attacks had reduced and she was coping better. As she was still somewhat anxious, the doctor suggested she take the remedies in pill form every fifteen minutes. By the time her wedding day arrived, Ginette was free of her fears, and was a calm, serene bride.

Bach Flower Remedies for children

The same unconventional doctor also discovered that children respond well to these gentle remedies. One very anxious young mother brought her 20-month-old son to the surgery. Ever since a fall from his cot two months earlier, the little boy's character had changed, and he was no longer happy and contented, but "cranky, nervous, and not sleeping." After ensuring that the child had no physical symptoms, either as a result of the fall or from some other non-related illness, the doctor concluded that the behavioral problems were the result of the shock of the fall. He suggested that the child be given four drops of Star of Bethlehem (for shock) in his drinks. Two days later, the child was back to his normal sunny self.

Crystals

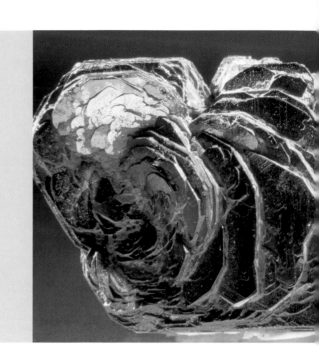

Crystals are widely used nowadays by healers and crystal therapists as a powerful tool for healing; they work on the body's subtle energy, helping to harmonize the body-mind system. Different kinds of crystal have different and specific healing qualities, but all crystals have two properties: they absorb negative vibrations, and they focus and enhance your thoughts and intentions.

When buying a crystal, use your intuition and allow yourself to be drawn to the right one for you. Since they absorb vibrations from other people, crystals should be cleansed after purchase, and also when they are "working"—either under cold running water or by soaking them in a bowl of water with a small amount of sea-salt. Leave them to dry for a few hours in sunlight or moonlight, which will also reenergize them. Once cleansed, you can dedicate your crystals to particular uses—relaxation, meditation, protection, and so on.

For relaxation and serenity, the following crystals may be helpful:

AGATE
Has a calming effect, and increases
vitality and confidence.

AMETHYST
Good for developing one's spiritual side.
Dispels fear and anxiety. Good for
insomnia, and for healing addictions.

APACHE TEARS
Releases inner pain and fear.

CALCITE
Helps release compulsive behavior.

CITRINE
Good for lack of confidence.
Helps build courage and self-esteem.
Removes emotional blocks and fears.

CLEAR QUARTZ
Balances energy, and supports the
immune system. Clears mood blocks,
facilitates clear thinking. Protects from
negative influences.

GREEN FLUORITE
Calms the nervous system, aids clear
thinking, and combats depression.

INDIGO SAPPHIRE
Excellent for mental problems, sadness,
muddled thinking, and insomnia.

JADE
Calming, healing, and balancing.

LAPIS LAZULI
Balances blood pressure. Aids creativity
and intuition.

ROSE QUARTZ
The stone for the heart center,
encouraging love for oneself and others.
Calms hyperactivity and anger, and
soothes anxiety and sadness.

SMOKY QUARTZ
Clears negativity, freeing the mind from
unwanted thoughts and fearfulness.
Improves self-esteem. Grounding.

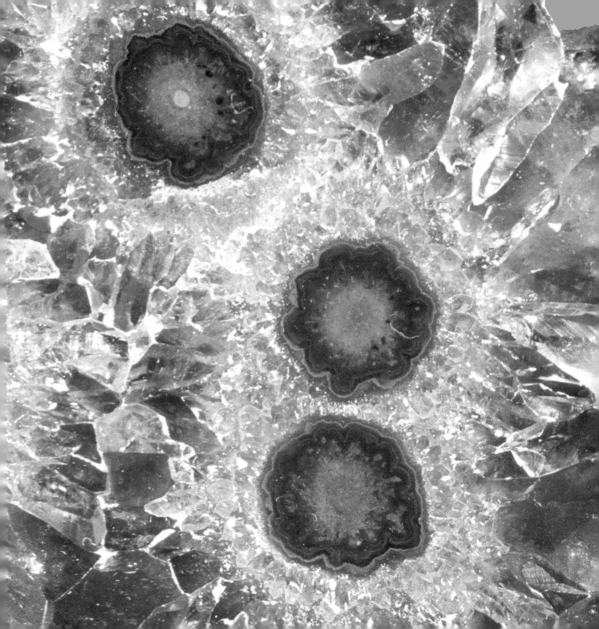

The power
of sound

Are you aware of the effect of sound on your system? A good way to recognize this is to imagine a movie without the music—the romance would seem less romantic, the frightening less fearful, and the drama less dramatic without the powerful sound that goes with it.

Sound has been used to aid healing since ancient times: African and Native American cultures use drums to cure sickness or induce altered states of consciousness, and the power of sound has long been recognized in the East. Overtone chanting has been brought to the West by a few pioneers; these remarkable harmonic sounds have been used by Tibetan monks for healing illness for thousands of years.

Today, music is used as a therapy in some hospitals and psychiatric units, and in the alternative field people are offering specialist workshops on sound of various kinds—like the magical sounds of Tibetan bowls.

Everything in the universe vibrates at particular frequencies, including the human body. The theory is that the right frequency of sound can therefore help to harmonize any disturbances in the body and mind. In fact, recent research has found that music with a pulse of about 60 beats a minute (which includes light classical music, New Age and ambient sounds) has a specific effect on the brainwaves, slowing them down from the beta-waves of ordinary consciousness to the alpha waves associated with relaxation.

Listening to relaxing music can calm the breathing, lift the spirits, reduce the heart rate, and lower the blood pressure. It can also help you to concentrate while working or studying. And some dentists are using it to relax and soothe their patients, with good effects.

We all have our own tastes in music, and what's totally relaxing for one person can be an irritant for another. But you can add to the effect of your regular relaxation sessions by choosing the music that is right for you. Experiment by noticing the effects of different types of music—gentle or uplifting orchestral or choral works, jazz, a single instrument, modern vocal by your favorite singer, or Gregorian chant from the medieval monasteries. Try other sounds, too: like the sound of the sea or the rainforest, something that brings back a happy memory, or the extraordinary vibrations of Tibetan bowls. Have a look in New Age shops for other soundtracks specially created to enhance meditation and relaxation. And look out for workshops teaching the use of the voice.

Start to become aware of what sound does, and doesn't, do for you. In this modern age, there is very often constant traffic noise, or a TV or radio playing, so remember, now and again, that there is relaxation to be found in the sound of silence.

Herbal
remedies
and teas

Although people may assume that herbal remedies are completely safe because they are "natural," they should be approached with caution. Chinese herbalism and the Medical Herbalism practiced in the West are forms of medicine requiring years of training and a wide knowledge. Some herbs can be harmful if wrongly prescribed, or may have a bad effect when combined with ordinary medication, so self-dosing is not recommended.

You can find herbal tranquilizers and sleeping pills in health stores, which are on the whole safe (though Valerian, which is an ingredient of many of these, does not suit everyone). However, like other pills, these treat the symptoms of stress, depression, or insomnia rather than the causes, and it is always better to explore the root of such problems—these are both conditions that may be alleviated by following a regular relaxation routine.

An exception is St John's Wort, which has become a popular alternative to antidepressants, and is recommended by some doctors. Another popular remedy is Kava-Kava; extracted from a Polynesian root. It is said to keep the mind both calm and clear, and is non-addictive. (Don't take it if you are pregnant, breastfeeding, or taking sedative medication.)

Herbal teas are quite safe (unless you have a particular allergy to any of the ingredients). They are an excellent substitute for caffeine, which can be overarousing (see page 236). For soothing the system, try camomile, lime flower, or lemon balm. If you have a lemon balm plant in your garden you can use the fresh leaves; pour boiling water on them and infuse for 4–5 minutes. Camomile is good for settling the digestion, and is an excellent alternative to coffee in the evening as it also promotes sound sleep.

Food
and drink

When we are tense or pressurized, it's only too easy to reach for instant comfort or convenience foods (like chocolate, cakes, burgers, and french fries) and give in to our addictions (such as caffeine and nicotine). Unfortunately, though these may give us an instant lift, they quickly let us down again, and do us no favors in the long run—they may actually cause stress by overworking the body without giving back good value in nutritional terms.

A healthier lifestyle will give you more energy, so that you are better able to cope with the stresses of everyday living—in time you will feel less need for that quick boost. Start by basing your diet on a wide variety of fresh whole foods, and include a raw salad with at least the recommended five daily servings of fresh fruit and vegetables a day. Go for wholegrain bread and pasta, brown rice rather than white, and replace white sugar with honey. By and large, keep your protein intake down—too much protein leaches minerals and trace elements from the body. According to some nutritionists, 3–4 ounces of fish or meat a day is plenty for most people, particularly if they also include plenty of wholegrains (rice, buckwheat, barley, wholewheat, and oats), pulses (lentils and beans), nuts and seeds in their diet.

Spring water

These days we are recommended to drink eight glasses of water a day—preferably spring water—exclusive of other drinks. The human body is composed of 70% water, and needs to keep hydrated. Both our muscles and our brains benefit from plenty of water, and drinking water when you are tired or stressed will actually give you far more of a lift than coffee or alcohol.

Allergies and addictions

More and more people are discovering that they are sensitive to certain types of foods or drinks—the most common are sugar, wheat, and dairy products, but other culprits include highly processed foods, shellfish, nuts, and even some fruits and vegetables. If you do have an allergy to any of these, it can affect your mood as well as your health, by overproducing adrenaline which makes you irritable and bad-tempered. Many children become hyperactive after overindulging in sugary foods and drinks, including cola drinks, which contain caffeine as well as very high sugar levels.

Very often we are addicted to the foods and drinks that we are allergic to: this is because these substances kick our adrenals into action, giving us a temporary lift. This overstimulation then leads to a dip in energy, and a craving for more of the same thing.

If you suspect you have an allergy or sensitivity, the best way to find out is to keep a diet diary for a week, and see if any patterns emerge—you may be able to see straight away that certain foods cause fatigue, irritability, or other symptoms. Cut the food or drink concerned out of your diet for a couple of weeks and see what happens. You may suffer mild or even severe withdrawal symptoms for a few days, such as headaches or constipation, and this is a good indication that your suspicions were right; but once your system is free of a damaging substance you will feel increasingly healthy and energized, calmer and happier.

If you have already introduced regular relaxation into your life, together with the concept of listening to your body, you may already be aware of the foods and drinks that are doing you no good. Keeping up a relaxation program will help you to change your habits.

Wheat and dairy products

You may well benefit from giving up wheat and dairy (cow's milk) products, which can be affecting you unawares; they may be exacerbating aches and pains and/or digestive problems, including constipation. There are plenty of good alternatives to wheat and cow's milk. Try substituting wheat with rye bread, rye biscuits, and rice cakes, and cow's milk products with soya milk, goat cheese, and goat or sheep yogurt.

Caffeine

Caffeine, particularly in the form of coffee, is the biggest no-no if you want to stay free of stress—many people are addicted to coffee without realizing it. Caffeine is also contained in cola drinks, tea, some "energy" drinks, chocolate, and painkillers.

Although it gives you a quick lift, regular intake of caffeine can produce serious long-term fatigue. It is a drug that stimulates the central nervous system, causes the heart to beat more rapidly, produces excess stomach acid, and raises the blood pressure. Too much can make you think less clearly. Caffeine overstimulates the adrenal glands, raising the levels of the stress hormones adrenaline and cortisol and thus reducing our ability to cope with stress. It overworks the pancreas, leading to the overproduction of insulin, which lowers the blood-sugar levels and leads to fatigue. In addition, it blocks the absorption of important nutrients like the B vitamins. It is a diuretic (overworking the kidneys and resulting in dehydration), and is believed to exacerbate pain.

In place of coffee and tea, try fruit juices, vegetable juice, dandelion coffee, and herbal teas, and remember to drink plenty of water.

Sugar

Sugar can also overstimulate the adrenal glands and weaken the immune system. We can get the natural sugar that we need in fresh and dried fruit and root vegetables, and energy from carbohydrates such as wholegrains. Use honey as a substitute in drinks or cooking; fresh or dried fruit poached in honey and water is delicious.

Alcohol

Alcohol is another adrenaline producer, and heavy consumption puts a strain on the liver and the kidneys, which have to overwork to process it through the body. It is also a diuretic (which is why we feel dehydrated after drinking a lot), and depletes many vitamins and minerals. Try limiting yourself to four measures a week. The rest of the time stick to tomato juice and fruit drinks.

Nicotine

While on the subject of addictions, a word should be said about smoking, which also has powerful effects on body and mind. Everyone knows the obvious dangers of smoking, particularly in relation to cancer, yet it is very hard to convince oneself to give it up.

People who smoke believe that it relaxes them—but does it really? The sense of relaxation from smoking a cigarette is simply the temporary satisfaction created by feeding an addiction. When you smoke, you are not just putting smoke and tar into your lungs, you are filling your bloodstream with harmful chemicals, including nicotine, which is a stimulant. This increases the heart rate, and in time can increase the likelihood of a heart attack or stroke. (And of course, to the addict, simply finding oneself without a cigarette can be an enormous cause of stress!)

Giving up smoking is for most people a stressful event, and smokers will come up with all sorts of reasons not to give up—fear of gaining weight is often a good excuse, although the fact that the smoker will save money is usually overlooked! It can be made easier by making a wholehearted decision to stop (rather than constantly telling yourself "I really should stop—some time"); and in fact, as we have seen, some people following a relaxation program may find themselves stopping spontaneously.

Write down all the reasons you personally have for stopping, set a date to give up, and until then, be very aware of all the effects that cigarettes have on your body and brain, how it affects your breathing and so on. Cut down by the simple expedient of telling yourself, "I don't need this now." When you do give up, give yourself full credit and all the relaxing treats you can.

Vitamins and minerals

Ideally, we should be taking in all the nutrients we need in our daily diet. However, most of us do not live on unpolluted organic farms where we can grow our vegetables and harvest them to serve completely fresh at every mealtime; even the "fresh fruits" we buy with the weekly shopping have probably traveled a long way to get to us, and will have lost some of their vitamin content in the process, while the vegetable and fruit peel that contain vitamin C may also have been sprayed with pesticides. To keep stress at bay, you may benefit from adding some or all of the following supplements to your diet. Always buy good-quality supplements.

VITAMIN C is naturally contained in all vegetables and fruit, especially citrus fruit. Broccoli and kiwi fruit contain particularly high levels. Since we don't store or manufacture it in the body, we need to make sure that we get some daily to keep the immune system strong and stave off infections.

RECOMMENDED DAILY INTAKE: 500–1000 MG.

MAGNESIUM AND CALCIUM are minerals that work together on our nervous system, and need to be taken in combination. They can help to reduce muscular cramps, migraines, and high blood pressure. Magnesium is believed by some nutritionists to be a good defense against cancer. Calcium is of course essential to healthy teeth and bones. Natural combinations of the two are found in seeds and fresh nuts, as well as in green leafy vegetables.

RECOMMENDED DAILY INTAKE: 100–250 MG OF EACH, EITHER SEPARATELY OR IN A READYMADE COMBINATION.

The range of B VITAMINS help to maintain the nervous system and produce energy. Vitamin B6 benefits some women who suffer from premenstrual tension. Again, a daily supply is necessary to good health. They are naturally contained in wholegrains, leafy vegetables, yogurt, tuna, oily fish like mackerel, avocado, beans, and yeast extract. RECOMMENDED DAILY INTAKE: 50 MG OF A GOOD COMBINATION B.

ZINC plays a part in manufacturing the adrenal hormones and in cell repair, and is depleted by stress. Lack of zinc has been associated with depression and low energy. It occurs naturally in seeds, lentils, nuts, whole grains, dark green vegetables, and seafood. RECOMMENDED DAILY INTAKE: 10–15 MG.

Take advice about suitable supplements if you are in any doubt.

relaxation in everyday life

> ❝Live as if each day would be your last
> Farm as if you would live to be a hundred.❞
>
> *Old country saying*

Some stress is necessary to life—there's no way of avoiding it. Even the most relaxed person is faced with difficulties and crises, and the adrenaline rush that spurs us to action is an essential part of our makeup. The damage is caused by prolonged, unresolved stress—but we all have the power to deal with this by changing our own behavior, attitudes, and responses, and our own sense of self.

Practicing a regular, deep form of relaxation can bring about changes in the nervous system, resulting in changed responses to daily situations. These include taking time before plunging into activity, living in the present moment, finding greater pleasure in one's relationships and environment, dropping compulsive and addictive behavior, improved self-esteem and self-trust, and an enhanced awareness of who you are and what you want out of life.

Incorporating these elements into your life may demand a degree of honest self-appraisal. Making time for a few minutes' relaxation every day is one thing—and it can be very beneficial. But deciding to adopt a relaxed approach in your daily living requires taking stock of your lifestyle, and perhaps introducing some changes. Human beings are creatures of habit, and often resistant to change—but "If you always do what you've always done, you'll always get what you've always got!"

The value of planning

The skilled archer takes time in drawing back the bowstring and taking careful aim: only then does he release the arrow so that it can fly straight to its destination.

When one is very busy or stressed, the temptation is to dive into the next activity without pause for thought—sometimes missing one's target altogether. It's when you rush into things that you make mistakes, lose papers and your temper, and spend hours looking for that vital number you wrote on a cleaning ticket.

However busy you are, a few minutes a day spent on planning your life are a few minutes that pay dividends. Planning ahead on paper, or on screen, enables you to see exactly what needs to be done and when, and also whether your aims are realistic.

Organize
your time

To help organize your time, it really is useful to make a list of everything that has to be done on a weekly and daily basis—it's also very satisfying to tick off each item as it's done. Some people are habitual listmakers—but making the list is only half the battle: it's only useful if you make it work for you. That means noting tasks that are top priority, those that are medium priority, and those that can wait, and dealing with them accordingly.

Alongside to-do lists, I find it very useful to timetable my days and weeks (even if it is rather reminiscent of school!). You may not stick to it rigidly, but it will give a structure to your day which you can see laid out in front of you.

Try making a timetable for your next week, including not just work but your spare time. Divide your time into hourly or half-hourly blocks, and fill these in in conjunction with your to-do list, scheduling in the jobs you have decided to do. Use a different colored pen for different types of activity, and include not only work but your social life, relaxation and exercise sessions, family life, and domestic chores. Make a point of leaving some time unscheduled, not just for emergencies, but so that you have the option of doing exactly what you feel like from time to time. If your hours are already fully filled in, you need to consider whether you are trying to pack in too much, and whether anything can be attended to at a later date or time.

Now take note of which colors predominate. Ideally, life should be a good balance of work, play, and rest. Are your working hours taking over all your timeslots? Could you be giving more time to play, rest, social life, and relationships? If you are missing out on these, what changes could you make? Play about with your timetable and see how you could manage your time more enjoyably.

Here are some points to bear in mind:

✿ When you schedule tasks into your timetable, allow for the fact that most things are likely to take longer than you think they will.

✿ If there's a task you've been putting off for some reason, schedule it in as if it is an appointment with someone else—and make sure you keep that appointment.

✿ Schedule in items not specifically to do with work but which need action—other people's birthdays, library-book return-by dates, car servicing, and so on.

✿ It's very useful to plan a catch-up day once a month—perhaps on a Saturday or Sunday—when you really will go through that pile of unread papers, or unwritten letters, or weed your e-mails, or deal with anything else that you have got behind with.

✿ Also schedule in a monthly treat for yourself.

Making your
plans happen

Some of us are wonderful at making lists and filling out time planners, but although we may have all the best intentions, somehow the plans don't get carried out, or not as completely as we'd like. There may be a number of reasons for this—we've taken on too much, we let ourselves be distracted or interrupted, or we just feel so overloaded we don't know where to start so we end up doing nothing at all.

Having a timetable should help, particularly if you schedule in relaxation times and treats to come when you've finished the day's work or chores. But after that, it's really up to you to make things happen, and once you discover how rewarding it is, you'll probably never look back. You will find it much easier to relax when all your chores are completed, and you'll probably find that your sleep is more restful too—there's nothing worse than waking with a jolt in the middle of the night because you've forgotten to do something.

Here are some suggestions for getting on with things smoothly:

❀ Focus on one task at a time, particularly if you're overwhelmed with problems hitting you from all sides. Don't try to tackle them all at once—you'll simply end up in a mental frazzle. Recognize that they're there, and that you can only deal effectively with one at a time. Take all the other problems, put them one at a time into an imaginary box, and close the lid firmly on each box until it's time to deal with them.

❀ Take your time—especially if you are under pressure—to read important letters or documents thoroughly before you respond to them, to read your own letters before you sign and post them, to check your to-do list, and to save vital documents on your computer. It's very easy to skip through things and make mistakes, and then have to spend time rectifying them.

❀ Be conscious of what you are doing now, however apparently trivial. It's when we are on automatic pilot, or thinking or worrying about something else, that we lose or forget keys, or leave an important document on public transport.

❀ By the same token, do have a place for everything and keep everything in its place. When we're in a rush we forget to put things back where they belong; looking for them later can waste time and energy. Take time to complete each activity by tidying up afterward. Walking into a tidy, uncluttered office or kitchen gives you a clean, relaxed start to your activities.

❀ Group together similar activities: if you have several phone calls to make, put some time aside and make them one after the other until they are all done. Save waffling time by writing a list beforehand of what you want to discuss with each person.

❧ Keep a notebook by the phone, at home, and at work, to write down anything you need to remember, including dates and phone numbers. This saves hours of hunting for that scrap of paper on which you wrote down something terribly important.

❧ Be prepared. Avoid last-minute panic by planning ahead: whether it's a journey, an evening out, or simply getting the children off to school, make whatever preparations you can in advance, the evening before if necessary. Always check your tickets the day before a journey.

❧ Look for ways in which you could be saving yourself time, such as shopping by Internet.

❧ Do it now! Try to deal with incoming mail as soon as it arrives, so that you don't need to read it twice. Similarly, file letters and documents away as soon as you've finished with them. There is nothing more daunting than a 6-inch high pile of filing—it's exhausting just to look at.

✿ If you really can't get everything done, then it may be that too many demands are being made of you. You may have to learn to say no. At work, delegate or ask for more help—if you're overloaded at home, you may need to ask a friend to help you. Discuss your workload with your boss, line manager, or partner. But don't let yourself get overloaded by trying to prove you're superhuman or being overanxious to please others. Sooner or later it will affect your performance and your health.

✿ Is there an item on your to-do list that keeps coming bottom of your priority list? Is it really low priority, or are you procrastinating for a reason—consciously or not? Make an effort to do the task and cross it off—you'll feel that you've really achieved something.

Procrastination

Procrastination is not just the thief of time, it is a cause of ongoing, niggling stress—stress induced both by resisting doing what we know we must, and by the consequent guilt of not having done it. You can, if you like, find yourself quite easily adding to the stress by beating yourself up about it.

It's a good idea, therefore, to make a firm decision to deal with whatever it is. This will probably entail facing up to the reason you have been putting it off. Is it because you don't feel up to that particular task? Is it something you simply dislike doing? Perhaps it involves having a discussion with someone you can't stand, or are angry with, or perhaps even a little scared of. Perhaps it's a visit to the dentist when you know that treatment is inevitable… Whatever it is, prolonging the agony of delay only makes it worse.

There is only one way to get over the discomfort, and that's by taking action. Make it top of your to-do list, schedule it in today, get help and advice if you need to—then just do it. And enjoy the feeling of relief and achievement when it's done.

It is important to understand what's underlying your delaying action, because there may actually be a good reason for it. If you are putting something off for negative reasons, you will have an associated physical discomfort when you think about it, probably in the solar plexus. But sometimes what feels like procrastination is a natural part of the gestation period that occurs before you make a big decision in life, and is a normal phase of the creative process. Your feelings about this will be different—but you may need to learn to distinguish between procrastination through fear or lack of confidence, and the self-trusting waiting that is genuinely creative.

Letting go

Letting go from time to time is an essential component of creativity, and as we learn to trust ourselves it can become a more and more useful tool. It is often during sleep that we come up with solutions to problems; and creative ideas can emerge when we are not looking for them. This happens when we switch off the active left brain, giving the creative right brain a chance—such as when we are out walking, or relaxing in the bath.

The creative process follows a natural cycle. There is the initial spark of an idea, followed by a period of planning, taking notes, acquiring information, and answering any self-doubts. Then comes a period of incubation, when the whole thing is handed over to the subconscious mind and that mysterious thing called inspiration starts working. This may at times feel like stuckness, but if you trust the process you will find that there comes a time when the project is ripe to bring to fruition. (Sometimes the initial spark is followed at once by a wonderful rush of creativity—but this has probably been preceded by a period of unconscious incubating below the surface.)

The creative process is not unlike the cyclical process of nature: the seed or bulb is planted in the earth and goes out of sight for a while. If it has been planted in good, well-prepared soil and is nurtured by the sun and rain, we can trust it to blossom at its own right time— and it can't be forced.

The creative process does not just apply to artistic endeavors. It may apply to a major work project, or to making an important life decision, like a change of jobs, careers, or home. During the incubation period our whole system may be gearing itself up for the move, even though we are not apparently taking action.

Listen to your body

Your body is very good at giving you clear messages about how it feels, what it needs, and when it has a problem, but when you're busy working, it's surprisingly easy to forget to listen, or to receive the message but choose to ignore it. Many people are sufficiently body-conscious to make time in the evenings for dancing, exercise, or relaxation, but ignore their body completely during their daily activities. Yet that's when it may really need your attention.

Practice becoming aware of your body language at all times, not just when your attention is focused on your body. If you're in the habit of rushing around at top speed, try slowing down a little. You'll feel calmer and more in control, and you'll find that other people respond to you more calmly too—tension is very catching.

❀ At work, are you putting unnecessary strains on your body? For a start, are you sitting comfortably? Are your chair, desk, and keyboard the right height for you? In most offices desks are all the same height, regardless of the height of the user. Your hands on the keyboard should be slightly lower than your elbows, but in many offices desks are much too high, which places unnecessary strain on the wrists, forearms, and shoulders.

❀ Your chair should be of a height that allows you to keep your feet flat on the floor. Crossing your legs or twisting the spine while sitting puts unnecessary pressure on the spinal cord and discs, and blocks the free flow of energy up the spine. So does holding the telephone receiver under your chin, which twists the neck and jaw. Your computer monitor should be directly in front of you at eye-level—if it's placed to one side this will ultimately cause neck strain.

❀ If you have to sit for long hours at work or study, do take breaks to move and walk around. If you've been sitting fixed in the same position for some time, make a point of adopting the opposite one for a minute or two: for example, if you have been rounding your shoulders over papers, take a break now and again to rotate the shoulders backwards.

❀ The shoulders can hold a lot of tension. Check them out at regular intervals: if they've crept up round your ears, let them drop consciously, breathing out at the same time.

❀ If you tend to hunch over a keyboard, try this technique for opening the chest and self-massaging the tight area between the shoulder blades. Stand facing the corner of a room and place your hands on each wall at ear level, with your feet about a foot behind your hands. Now bend your arms so that your body leans forward.

You will experience a satisfying stretch in your chest and a squeeze between the shoulder blades. If there is no furniture-free corner, do this in a doorway.

❀ Listen to your body in other ways, too, like noticing when you feel tired. Busy people often try to ignore and override fatigue, but in the long run this can only further deplete your energy. Take note, and take preventative action by having a relaxed evening and an early night. (Sometimes people who practice yoga or chi kung find they feel more tired after a class; this is because these techniques make you more aware of your body and your true state of being.)

❀ Notice what and how and when you are eating. How often do you eat or drink out of sheer habit, not because you're particularly hungry or thirsty? Conversely, if you're working very hard, do you neglect to eat? Be in tune with your own needs.

✿ Having said that, regular eating hours do help the body to cope. Your organs have their own timing, and the digestive system is at its most efficient in the morning, slowing down during the day, and especially in the late evening. Hence a good breakfast really does give a good start to your day, by turning food into energy more efficiently, whereas eating late at night forces your body to work much harder to get the best out of what you put into it, which can make you sluggish in the morning.

✿ Try to take a real break at lunchtime, and avoid eating at your desk or on the hoof, neither of which gives your digestion a chance to get the best out of food. Even if you only have a sandwich for lunch, eat it in a peaceful atmosphere, in a park or garden if the weather is fine. That way you will give your whole system a refreshing change of scene.

Beating stress

There are a number of things you can do to avoid building up stress and tension as you go about your day. They should also make life more enjoyable and manageable.

They might seem like little things, but simply remembering to take regular breaks or to breathe deeply will be really beneficial in helping you to keep a healthy, optimistic outlook on life.

If you're working very hard, whether at home or in a job, it's important to take a break now and again—to stretch, to move, to breathe, and to come back to yourself. Do it after finishing one task and before moving on to the next; it needn't take long, but during that time you can mentally assign the task you have completed to the "finished" pile and prepare yourself for the new task ahead.

One spiritually oriented organization encourages its staff to switch off completely for a minute once an hour—stopping whatever they're doing, letting the mind and body be quiet and still for that time.

If you're getting uptight, notice if your breathing has become shallow, or whether you are holding your breath. Place your awareness on your breathing and let it slow down naturally. My friend Susi devised a stress-beating exercise for herself, while on a self-development course. She told me: "When I get very stressed I get completely knotted up around the shoulders and the neck. So I take a really deep intake of breath, very, very slowly raising my arms to the sides parallel with the floor. As I let the breath out the shoulders automatically go down. Because the arms are stretched out, the lungs can take in and expel more breath. After doing this about four times I am completely calm."

There are many other techniques you can adopt to beat stress—keeping something symbolic of relaxation near you as you work is an excellent method; and concentrating completely on some physical task for a few minutes each day calms the mind and quiets the thoughts. Learn to deal with anxiety by discussing your problem with a friend or writing it down on paper—focusing your mind on it can sometimes bring a solution.

Try learning techniques for "grounding" yourself, and for emotional stress relief, or do what comes naturally and have a good cry—or a good laugh! Learn to give yourself regular treats, such as a massage or a relaxation weekend; this will reassure your body that you care for it.

Learn how to communicate effectively—with your partner, with colleagues, with your children. And finally, learn to accept yourself, and give yourself a pat on the back every day—you deserve it!

Remind yourself of peace and calm

Keep a picture or photograph of a scene that represents relaxation for you near your workstation or wherever you spend most of your time. It might be the sea, a sleeping animal, a country landscape, a river, an abstract that inspires serenity, or your favorite holiday spot. Look at it every now and then, and let your imagination enter the scene for a few moments—your mind will immediately associate the image with peace and calm.

If you prefer something tactile, use a rock, a large pebble, a crystal, or some other natural object as your calming symbol. Close your eyes for a few moments and tune in to its energy.

Stroking an animal has been shown to lower the blood pressure, and animals do seem to have an instinctive knowledge of when you are in need of a little comfort or stress relief. Cats are particularly soothing to stroke, and their rhythmic purring is very calming.

Practice living
in the present

Try to spend five minutes a day focusing purely on the present moment. This is most easily done while you are engaged in some form of physical activity—like walking, ironing, gardening, or doing the washing up. Let your attention be totally on the action: feel your feet as they touch the ground, or your hands as they handle plants or plates. Feel the texture of the fabric, or the sensation of the water. Be aware of all the sights, sounds, and sensations, and allow your mind to be completely quiet.

If you spend a lot of time staring at a computer screen, make a point of looking away at regular intervals, out of the window if possible. You can also rest your eyes by palming. Place the palms of your hands over your eyes, with your elbows comfortably supported. Close your eyes and let them be soothed and rested by the darkness and the warmth of your hands for about five minutes.

Deal with
anxiety

If you're worried or anxious, sitting on your problem and brooding about it won't help; if your mind is constantly revolving around the subject, try talking to a friend or colleague. But make sure that you are getting it out of your system and not simply talking yourself into a groove. Pick someone to talk to who you know will listen seriously and will give you feedback and perhaps constructive advice.

Alternatively, write your anxieties down on a piece of paper and put it away overnight. Have a look at what you've written next day, as objectively as you can. You may well come up with solutions you hadn't previously thought of.

Bear in mind, too, that when you are overtired, problems can look a lot bigger—if your thoughts are revolving on a treadmill, check out your fatigue level, and put the problem aside, if you can, until you are feeling more refreshed.

Emotional stress release

If you are feeling uptight, perhaps after a difficult encounter with someone, try this simple technique. It takes 1–10 minutes.

Place your fingers lightly on the bumps on your forehead halfway between the midline of your eyebrows and your hairline, while recalling the situation you are upset about. Run the detail of it through your mind. After a few minutes you will find it more difficult to focus on; you may also feel a pulse in the two points on your brow.

At this point, open your eyes, think again about the problem and see how you feel about it now. You should be able to view it much more calmly and objectively.

This works because the points on your brow have a connection with the stomach, where we feel anxiety. Holding them encourages blood supply to the stomach and the frontal lobes of the brain—the part which functions in present time and doesn't react to memory.

Have a good cry

Having a good cry can release an enormous amount of tension. Sometimes it's difficult on your own, but a kind and sympathetic friend can help to start you off! Crying releases tension in the ribs and diaphragm, while helping to off-load tension; it's also a way of releasing stress hormones, which have been found in tears.

Have a good giggle

Sometimes it's difficult to access your sense of humor, and losing it completely is a definite sign that you are over-stressed. But humor— so long as it's appropriate—can lighten a heavy day's work or a family crisis. And a really good laugh, or getting the giggles with a friend over something silly, is very healing. Laughter also releases all-over tensions and tight muscles in the diaphragm and lifts your mental energy.

Give yourself
a treat

At least once a month give yourself an in-depth experience of letting go and being cared for. Treat yourself to a facial and massage, a sauna, an alternative therapy treatment such as Shiatsu, or a session relaxing in the darkness of a flotation tank.

If you can afford it, take an occasional weekend break at a health farm, or try a residential weekend of meditation, yoga, t'ai chi, or chi kung, or maybe laughter therapy. Look out for one-day workshops as well, or go on a rambling or painting weekend.

If finances and time are limited, you can still give yourself a complete evening of self-nurturing, including self-massage, a facial, a bubble-bath, and a session of relaxation (for this one, you can lie on your bed). Light some candles, put your favorite aromatherapy oils in a vaporizer, and put on some relaxing music. And just enjoy the sensation of total liberation from time, obligations, and anxieties.

Self-massage

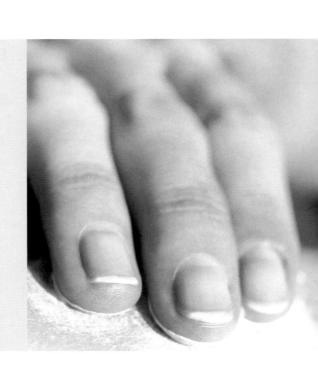

Although massaging oneself does not bring about the sense of complete indulgence and relaxation you get from being massaged by someone else, it can still be both calming and energizing. It's also an excellent way of letting your body know that you care for it.

You can use body lotion for a quick five-minute massage after your bath, or preferably take a little longer, using a few drops of your favorite aromatherapy oil, sweet almond oil for example. You can also buy all sorts of delicious ready-blended massage oils.

Never use undiluted essential oils. Take care over your choice of oil and get advice if you are pregnant, trying to get pregnant, or suffering from any medical condition. Don't use bergamot if you are going to be exposed to sunlight afterward.

There are no hard and fast rules for self-massage. Try out the following guidelines and experiment with what you find beneficial.

❀ Start by tapping lightly all over your scalp with your fingertips, keeping your wrists loose.

❀ Gently stroke down your face and neck toward your shoulders. Use your right hand to knead your left shoulder, and your left hand to knead the right. If you like, close your fist loosely and, keeping your wrist loose, tap your fist along and around each shoulder and your upper arms.

❀ Work your way down each arm, gently stroking, kneading, and tapping as feels best to you. As you reach your hands, stroke down and off each finger in turn, sensing that you are getting rid of stale energy and fatigue.

❀ Place your hands each side round your back just above your waist, and gently massage this area in a circular movement. This helps to stimulate the kidneys.

✿ Smooth your hands down your lower back. Use both hands to gently massage your sacrum (the large shield-shaped bone at the bottom of the spine.)

✿ Massage your abdomen with both hands flat, using a clockwise circular motion.

✿ Massage your hips and buttocks in a circular motion; try using your fingers, and then tap yourself with loosely clenched fists.

✿ Spend time on your thighs, kneading and gently pinching, back and front. Tap them with your fists. Then work your way down each leg, tapping down the outsides and insides. Use sweeping movements down your feet, and give attention to each toe—wiggle them between your fingers, then sweep off any fatigue and stale energy.

✿ To massage your back and spine, curl yourself into a ball, with your arms holding your knees, and roll from side to side a few times.

Centering
and grounding
yourself

Before undertaking something stressful, like an exam, a driving test, a job interview, or a difficult encounter at work, it is helpful to spend a few minutes centering and grounding yourself.

❀ Standing, take a few slow breaths and let any tension you are holding flow out of your body from your head to your toes. Let your face, jaw, and neck be relaxed, let your shoulders drop, and imagine any tension flowing out through your hands and your feet. Give your hands a shake.

❀ Close your eyes and sense yourself inside your body (not just in your head). Now think of a pole of light, in whatever color comes to you, flowing in through the top of your head, down through the center of your body, and deep into the earth. Sense your feet planted firmly on the floor, and imagine growing roots deep down into the earth.

❀ Now raise your arms sideways and above your head, and as you breathe in, visualize a stream of golden cosmic energy pouring into them. Fill your hands with this energy and on the outbreath bring them down to your heart, filling your heart with calm.

❀ Repeat this, this time bringing your hands down to your solar plexus, taking a moment to imagine the golden light filling it with courage.

❀ Repeat this a third time, bringing your hands down to your lower abdomen, filling it with golden light and strength.

❀ Feel any leftover tension draining down through your feet. Feel your feet firmly planted on the ground, supported by the energy of the earth. Keep breathing deeply and calmly for a moment or two.

❀ Now open your eyes and come back to the world ready to face the challenge.

Stress and other people

If you have good relationships with your colleagues at work, it can make up for a lot of dissatisfaction you may feel about your job. But it can be difficult to maintain calm when you're at the receiving end of stress-inducing behavior from others, either at home or at work. Probably the most common response to difficult colleagues or employers is to swallow one's feelings, rather than rock the boat by risking a confrontation—or to have a good moan with a friend in the lunch hour. Moaning unfortunately usually makes us feel worse, without altering anything. So what can you do?

You can only bring about change by communicating directly with the person or people causing problems. Remember that assertiveness is not the same thing as aggression, and everyone has the right to assert their needs. Practice assertiveness by explaining to your boss, for instance, that the workload he has given you is unrealistic, or that you cannot work late without prior notice.

If stress is coming from management—as is very often the case—you have three choices. You can put up with it and continue to increase your own stress levels; you can look for another job, which you may not wish to do; or you can try to get things changed. If you decide that this is the way forward, it is worth asking for a meeting with your employer or manager, and stating your case in as constructive a way as you can. You may find that your manager was unaware that you were having a problem and be delighted that you have raised it so that a mutually satisfactory solution can be found.

If there's a particular person at work or home whose behavior is making your life difficult—whether it's a colleague, your partner, or your roommate—you must decide whether you are going to put up with it, or tackle them. There are ways of doing this that are more or less effective. Sighing, dropping hints, slamming doors, and sulking are all indirect ways of communicating, which have little effect except possibly to irritate the other person, who will still ignore your signals, and you will feel even more frustrated. Blowing your top may relieve your feelings at the time, but no-one actually responds well to being shouted at. Nor do they necessarily hear what you are really saying, and are likely to put their own interpretation on your outburst.

It is possible to express your anger or irritation effectively without descending into a shouting match. Watch your body language—any feelings of aggression will come over only too clearly. Learning to communicate directly not only has the benefit of getting yourself heard; you'll find that it improves your self-esteem.

Effective communication

Don't tackle the other person while you're at boiling point. Cool down, then think what you want to say; you may find it helpful to write it down. Make it specific—don't draw up a list of lingering irritations.

Tell the other person you would like to have a talk with them, and pick a moment when it's convenient for both of you. State how their behavior affects you, very specifically—but do it without blaming. For example, rather than saying in a confrontational manner, "You're really difficult to work with, you're always criticizing me," tell them: "I felt hurt when you criticized my work in front of others this morning."

Give them a chance to reply, and show you are listening to their answer. If you can open up a dialog, you may get an apology and even a change in behavior. People are sometimes unaware how they are affecting others unless they get feedback. You may learn that they, too, are under stress, and you might find yourselves unexpectedly united.

Children
and stress

Children these days are subject to all kinds of stress. They are bombarded with stimuli from all sides, and expected to perform well educationally from an early age. A quarrel with a friend or bullying at school can cause a lot of unhappiness. And children are stressed by events such as bereavement or divorce, or the birth of a sibling.

Stress in children may manifest itself as "naughtiness", increased susceptibility to infections, bedwetting, headaches, sleep disturbances, mood swings, clinginess, stomach upsets, and picky eating. Try to spot what's happening, and open up good communications with your child—let them know that they have your support and love.

Older children may suffer from adult-weight stress; important exams come along at the same time as the hormonal changes that can seriously affect their mood. Bear this in mind when they are being moody, and give them as much encouragement as you can.

Know yourself
and be yourself

"This above all, to thine own self be true…."

William Shakespeare

A lot of tension is caused by trying to fit into other people's expectations and standards, through ambition, the desire to please, or a lack of self-awareness. Some people spend their entire working lives in the wrong job or profession because at some point they have opted for pleasing an ambitious parent, or have put the need to make money before job satisfaction. The more you can be true to yourself in your work and play, the happier and more relaxed you will be.

There are people who apparently thrive on stress and working till all hours—usually they also love what they are doing, and are in charge of it. If you are not one of these, don't try to be one. There is a culture of working long hours at present, despite the fact that research has shown that longer hours do not mean greater productivity or efficiency. Be aware of your own rhythms and energy levels and work to your own pace if you can.

Are you in the driving seat, or are you being driven? Do you spend your life pleasing yourself, or revolving around other people? A balanced life consists of a blend of the two. Totally selfish people are liable to run into conflict with others, but if you are giving away too much of yourself, the conflict will be experienced in your own body and mind. If you find it hard to say no, you could benefit from an assertiveness-training course.

How aware are you of your thinking patterns, and how you talk to yourself? What we think and speak feeds back into our unconscious mind, which then plays our words back for good or ill. Thoughts like, "I can't do this, I'll never get it done!" have an immediately lowering effect on the system, and become self-fulfilling prophecies. Try substituting these thoughts with more positive ones, like "I'll do my best to get this done." Negative thoughts may be a sign of lack of self-confidence and overfatigue, and may not actually reflect reality. Try to get a break, and try a Bach Flower Remedy—repetitive thoughts can be lifted with White Chestnut, and Larch is good for self-confidence.

It can take time to get to know yourself. From an early age our thoughts about life and about ourselves are conditioned by the views of the adults around us. Try to become aware of your thoughts and beliefs about yourself, and question how many of them are your truth.

Are you a perfectionist?

Perfectionism is a characteristic of Type A people—the people who drive themselves too hard. Hard-core perfectionists can cause a lot of stress not only to themselves but to those around them. Yet, quite clearly, nobody is absolutely perfect, and the world is never, ever going to be exactly the way you think it should be. The one thing perfectionists do to perfection is to find fault with themselves, the world, and other people. It doesn't make for happiness.

If you come into this category, you may have been born that way, or perfectionism may have been instilled into you. Ask yourself:

✿ Who told me I had to win every time?

✿ Who told me I had to be top in every exam?

✿ Who told me I was never allowed to make any mistakes?

✿ Why can I never allow myself to fail?

✿ Would the world come to an end if I did fail or make a mistake?

Think about your answers, and notice whether these characteristics are really part of your makeup, or whether they actually stem from high expectations imposed on you by others. Recognize that on the other side of the desire to achieve is the fear of failure, and fear is a major cause of stress. And remember when dealing with others that encouragement always brings out the best in people, while criticism rarely does—and when you see the positive reaction of the other person to your words, you will also discover that giving praise is every bit as rewarding as receiving it.

Adopting a more relaxed and less obsessively perfectionist approach to life does not mean becoming passive or inactive. Rather, it is a way of living that enables you to deal with things more calmly, more effectively, and with less strain and fatigue. Recognize that there is nothing shameful in failing now and again. In fact, there is often more to learn from failure than from success. Good friends will not judge us for failing; what makes other people like or love us is not based on high achievement.

In any case, it's quite likely that your ideas of perfection may not be the same as other people's. I once had a roommate who would fly into a rage if I complained that she wasn't doing her share, and I assumed that this was because she didn't like to be thought of as lazy; then she admitted one day that it was because she couldn't bear not to be thought of as perfect! To me, the perfect roommate or friend is someone who can admit to their imperfections!

If you believe that your self-image depends on impressing other people with your performance, that actually makes you very vulnerable. True self-esteem means accepting yourself for who you really are, warts and all.

Take it easy
on yourself

How we perceive the world depends very much on where we place our attention. It's terribly easy to focus just on what's wrong—with events, with the world, with other people, and with yourself. As you go through your day, try noticing the good things. They might be quite small—a blackbird singing in the garden, the enthusiasm of a toddler learning about the great wide world—or more important, like someone praising you for a piece of work well done. Whatever they are, take them in. Our thoughts and attitudes affect our body and our energy, and happy thoughts can be very healing.

Spend a few minutes last thing at night mentally going over your day. Recall all the things that went right, or that you enjoyed, however small. Give yourself a pat on the back for any achievements. You will probably find that this helps you feel physically different—calmer and lighter—as well as in a contented mood in which to drift off to sleep.

Go with
the flow

Take care of the present moment, and the future will take care of itself. To be relaxed means to be at peace with oneself, which enables us to be more at peace with the rest of the world. Far from being a self-indulgence, being fully in tune with yourself will enable you better to fulfill the needs of others when it's appropriate. When you feel yourself getting caught up in tension or anxiety, or giving way to an habitual negative response, just come back to yourself, to your center. Stop for a minute, breathe, and let go of any tension in your body.

Practicing a regular relaxation technique results in a fuller and more satisfying life. Harmonizing the two sides of the brain enhances intuition and creativity, and in the long term enables you to develop an increased sense of self-trust and self-worth. The end result can be a greater pleasure in life, in your work and playtime, and in your relationships with others and with yourself.

Acknowledgments

I would like to thank all those who have generously contributed their time and information to this book, including Vera Diamond, Judy Hammond, Izzy Harrap, Delcia McNeil, Elizabeth St John, The Mary Ward Centre, Renate Lalloo, Tanja Raaste, Ilona Tate, Glyn Williams, and Susan Winton-Lyle.

Further reading

Barbara Brown & Günter Knöferl, *Qi Gong: The Chinese art of working with energy*, Thorsons, HarperCollins, London 2001

Don Campbell, *The Mozart Effect*, Hodder & Stoughton, London, 2001

Dr Vernon Coleman, *How to Conquer Backache*, Hamlyn, Reed Consumer Books Ltd, London, 1993

Ursula Fleming, *Grasping the Nettle: A positive approach to pain*, Collins, Fount Paperbacks, London, 1990

Clare G Harvey and Amanda Cochrane, *The Encyclopedia of Flower Remedies*, Thorsons, HarperCollins, London 1995

Soozi Holbeche, *The Power of Gems and Crystals: How they can transform your life*, Piatkus, London, 1989

Neil Irwin, *Crystals*, Thorsons, London, 2000

Maggie La Tourelle with Anthea Courtenay, *Thorsons Principles of Kinesiology*, Thorsons, HarperCollins, London 1992

Lawrence LeShan, *How to Meditate: A guide to self-discovery*, Thorsons, HarperCollins, London, 1983

Leslie Kenton, *10 Day De-stress Plan: Make stress work for you*, Ebury Press, London, 1994

Joel Levey and Michelle Levey, *Simple Meditation and Relaxation*, Conari Press, Berkeley, California, 1999

Delcia McNeil, *Bodywork Therapies for Women: A guide*, The Women's Press Ltd, London, 2000

Jane Madders, *Relax and Be Happy: Techniques for 5–18 year olds*, Unwin, London, 1987

Michael Tse, *Qigong for Health and Vitality*, Piatkus, London, 1995

index